Casual Cookouts includes:

- 65 recipes for meat, poultry, fish and seafood, vegetarian entrées, side dishes, and desserts
- All recipes tested and approved in the Better Homes and Gardens® Test Kitchen
- Serving suggestions with each entrée
- Grilling charts for meat, poultry, fish and seafood, and vegetables
- Preparation and grilling times
- Nutrition information with every recipe

Better Homes and Gardens®

fresh

series

Put the fresh back into dinnertime with these additional books in the *Fresh and Simple*™ series by Better Homes and Gardens® Books.

Better Homes and Gardens®

fresh and simple™

casual cookouts

Better Homes and Gardens® Books

Des Moines, Iowa

All of us at Better Homes and Gardens® Books
are dedicated to providing you with the information and ideas you need to create delicious foods. We welcome your comments and suggestions. Write to us at: Better Homes and Gardens® Books, Cookbook Editorial Department, LN-112, 1716 Locust St., Des Moines, IA 50309–3023.

If you would like to purchase additional copies of any of our books, check wherever books are sold.

Our seal assures you that every recipe in *Casual Cookouts* has been tested in the Better Homes and Gardens® Test Kitchen. This means that each recipe is practical and reliable, and meets our high standards of taste appeal. We guarantee your satisfaction with this book for as long as you own it.

Pictured on front cover: Veal Chops with Pesto-Stuffed Mushrooms (see recipe, *page 14*)
Pictured on page 1: Dilly Salmon Fillets (see recipe, *page 52*)

Better Homes and Gardens® Books
An imprint of Meredith® Books

Fresh and Simple™ Casual Cookouts
Editor: Lisa Holderness
Project Editor and Writer: Lisa Kingsley
Contributing Editors: Nancy Verde Barr, Jennifer Darling, Karen Levin, Joan Moravek, Spectrum Communication Services, Inc.
Designer: Craig Hanken
Copy Chief: Catherine Hamrick
Copy and Production Editor: Terri Fredrickson
Contributing Copy Editor: Jennifer Speer Ramundt
Contributing Proofreaders: Gretchen Kaufmann, Susan J. Kling, Beth Popplewell
Contributing Indexer: Martha Fifield
Electronic Production Coordinator: Paula Forest
Editorial and Design Assistants: Judy Bailey, Treesa Landry, Karen Schirm
Test Kitchen Director: Sharon Stilwell
Test Kitchen Product Supervisor: Marilyn Cornelius
Food Stylists: Lynn Blanchard, Janet Pittman
Photographers: Jim Krantz, Kritsada Panichgul
Prop Stylist: Karen Johnson
Production Director: Douglas M. Johnston
Production Manager: Pam Kvitne
Assistant Prepress Manager: Marjorie J. Schenkelberg

Meredith® Books
Editor in Chief: James D. Blume
Design Director: Matt Strelecki
Managing Editor: Gregory H. Kayko

Director, Sales & Marketing, Retail: Michael A. Peterson
Director, Sales & Marketing, Special Markets: Rita McMullen
Director, Sales & Marketing, Home & Garden Center Channel: Ray Wolf
Director, Operations: George Susral

Vice President, General Manager: Jamie L. Martin

Better Homes and Gardens® Magazine
Editor in Chief: Jean LemMon
Executive Food Editor: Nancy Byal

Meredith Publishing Group
President, Publishing Group: Christopher M. Little
Vice President, Consumer Marketing & Development: Hal Oringer

Meredith Corporation
Chairman and Chief Executive Officer: William T. Kerr

Chairman of the Executive Committee: E. T. Meredith III

contents

get outdoors & get grilling!

Grilling out just got more exciting. These days, a meal cooked over the coals means more than just meat. *Fresh and Simple*™ *Casual Cookouts* features dinners loaded with fresh and flavorful produce, seasonings, and herbs. The results will send your family dashing to your outdoor dining room as soon as they catch the aromas wafting from the grill. Take advantage of menus that can be cooked entirely on the grill, and serve up wholesome foods that are anything but predictable. *Casual Cookouts* helps you move the weeknight kitchen or the Saturday night party outdoors so you can savor great food, good company, and fresh air.

fire up for
beef, pork, and lamb

grilled beef, red onion, & blue cheese salad

The natural sweetness of red onions is intensified when the onions are brushed with a balsamic vinaigrette and grilled alongside sirloin steak. Aromatic grilled herb bread makes a perfect go-along to this crisp and hearty main-dish salad.

Prep: 15 minutes   Grill: 8 minutes   Makes 4 servings

For vinaigrette, in a screw-top jar combine oil, vinegar, garlic, ½ teaspoon salt, and ½ teaspoon pepper; cover and shake well. Trim fat from steak. Remove 1 tablespoon vinaigrette from jar and brush evenly onto both sides of steak. Press thyme and rosemary onto both sides of the steak. Brush both sides of onion slices with some of the remaining vinaigrette, reserving the rest; set aside.

Grill steak on rack of an uncovered grill directly over medium heat to desired doneness, turning once. (Allow 8 to 12 minutes for medium-rare and 12 to 15 minutes for medium doneness.) For last 10 minutes of grilling, place onions on grill rack beside meat. Grill onions until tender, turning once.

Divide mesclun among 4 dinner plates. To serve, thinly slice the steak across the grain. Separate onion slices into rings. Arrange warm steak and onions atop mesclun. Drizzle with the reserved vinaigrette. Top with cheese and tomatoes.

Nutrition facts per serving: 266 cal., 16 g total fat (5 g sat. fat), 59 mg chol., 373 mg sodium, 9 g carbo., 2 g fiber, 22 g pro. Daily values: 7% vit. A, 28% vit. C, 4% calcium, 22% iron

- 2 **tablespoons olive oil**
- 3 **tablespoons balsamic vinegar**
- 1 **clove garlic, minced**
- 1 **boneless beef sirloin steak, cut 1 inch thick (about ¾ pound)**
- 1 **tablespoon snipped fresh thyme**
- 2 **teaspoons snipped fresh rosemary**
- 4 **¼-inch-thick slices red onion**
- 6 **cups lightly packed mesclun or torn mixed salad greens**
- 2 **tablespoons crumbled Gorgonzola or blue cheese**
- 8 **yellow and/or red pear tomatoes, halved**

Serving suggestion:

While you're enjoying this salad, put Nectarine-Raspberry Crisp (page 83) on the grill for dessert.

steak rémoulade sandwiches

Served in France as an accompaniment to cold meats, fish, and seafood, the classic mayonnaise-based sauce called rémoulade adds a hint of rustic sophistication to this steak sandwich perked up by peppery arugula and grilled sweet peppers.

8

¼ **cup light mayonnaise dressing or salad dressing**

1½ **teaspoons finely minced cornichons or gherkins**

1 **teaspoon capers, chopped**

¼ **teaspoon lemon juice**

2 **8-ounce boneless beef loin strip steaks**

2 **teaspoons prepared garlic spread or 2 teaspoons bottled minced garlic**

1 **large yellow sweet pepper, seeded and cut lengthwise into 8 strips**

4 **kaiser or French-style rolls, split**

1 **cup arugula or spinach leaves**

Serving suggestion:

Accompany this hearty sandwich with crisp purchased coleslaw and baked potato chips.

Prep: 15 minutes   Grill: 8 minutes   Makes 4 servings

For rémoulade, in a small bowl combine mayonnaise dressing, cornichons, capers, lemon juice, and a pinch freshly ground black pepper. Cover and refrigerate until needed.

Pat steaks dry with a paper towel. Rub garlic spread over steaks. Sprinkle with additional freshly ground black pepper. Grill steaks and sweet pepper strips on rack of an uncovered grill directly over medium heat until meat is desired doneness, turning once. (Allow 8 to 12 minutes for medium-rare and 12 to 15 minutes for medium doneness.) Transfer cooked steaks and sweet pepper strips to a cutting board; cut steaks into ¼-inch-thick slices.

If desired, grill rolls directly over medium heat about 1 minute or until toasted. Spread rémoulade on bottom halves of rolls; top with arugula, steak slices, sweet pepper, and roll tops.

Nutrition facts per serving: 380 cal., 13 g total fat (3 g sat. fat), 65 mg chol., 516 mg sodium, 37 g carbo., 0 g fiber, 29 g pro. Daily values: 2% vit. A, 144% vit. C, 6% calcium, 29% iron

jerk london broil

Got a hankering for a little heat? The small Scotch bonnet pepper—one of the hottest peppers on the planet and a star in Jamaican cooking—packs a powerful punch. If you can't find a Scotch bonnet or want less heat, substitute a jalapeño pepper.

Prep: 10 minutes **Marinate:** Up to 24 hours
Grill: 12 minutes **Makes 6 servings**

For jerk marinade, combine all ingredients except steak in a blender container; cover and blend until smooth. Diagonally score both sides of the steak at 1-inch intervals, making a diamond pattern. Place the steak in a glass dish; spread the marinade over the steak. Grill right away or cover steak with plastic wrap and marinate in the refrigerator for up to 24 hours.

Grill the steak on the rack of an uncovered grill directly over medium heat to desired doneness, turning once. (Allow 12 to 14 minutes for medium doneness.) Transfer the steak to a cutting board; cut across the grain into ⅛- to ¼-inch-thick slices.

Nutrition facts per serving: 187 cal., 11 g total fat (3 g sat. fat), 44 mg chol., 117 mg sodium, 2 g carbo., 0 g fiber, 18 g pro. Daily values: 4% vit. A, 8% vit. C, 1% calcium, 13% iron

- 4 **green onions**
- 1 **1-inch piece fresh ginger, sliced**
- 1 **Scotch bonnet pepper, stem and seeds removed (optional)**
- 2 **tablespoons cooking oil**
- 3 **cloves garlic**
- 2 **teaspoons Jamaican jerk seasoning**
- ¼ **cup lime juice**
- 1 **1¼- to 1½-pound beef flank steak**

Serving suggestion:

Top off this island-style steak with a side of Sweet & Spicy Pepper-Pineapple Salsa (page 75).

this **jerk** is all **wet**

Jerk seasoning—a powerful and pungent spice mixture of chile peppers, thyme, cinnamon, ginger, allspice, and cloves—is most often used as a dry rub for meats. But jerk can be "wet," too. That simply means the jerk spices—along with onions and/or garlic—are mixed with some kind of liquid to make a marinade.

sun-dried tomato burgers

Burgers on the grill take on a whole new meaning when they're infused with fresh lemon, studded with dried tomatoes, and slathered with a basil mayonnaise dressing zipped up with a jalapeño pepper.

11

Prep: 15 minutes   Grill: 14 minutes   Makes 4 servings

In a medium bowl combine beef, tomatoes, lemon peel, ½ teaspoon salt, and ¼ teaspoon pepper; mix lightly but thoroughly. Shape into four ½-inch-thick patties. Grill patties on the rack of an uncovered grill directly over medium heat for 14 to 18 minutes or until no pink remains, turning once.

Meanwhile, in a small bowl combine mayonnaise dressing, basil, and jalapeño pepper; mix well. For the last 1 to 2 minutes of grilling, place buns, cut sides down, on grill rack to toast. Top bottom halves of buns with burgers. Top with mayonnaise dressing mixture and arugula. Add bun tops.

Nutrition facts per serving: 450 cal., 20 g total fat (6 g sat. fat), 71 mg chol., 784 mg sodium, 40 g carbo., 2 g fiber, 26 g pro. Daily values: 1% vit. A, 13% vit. C, 6% calcium, 25% iron

1 **pound lean ground beef**

1 **tablespoon finely chopped, drained, oil-packed sun-dried tomatoes**

1 **teaspoon finely shredded lemon or lime peel**

¼ **cup light mayonnaise dressing or salad dressing**

2 **tablespoons snipped fresh basil**

1 **jalapeño pepper, seeded and finely chopped**

4 **onion hamburger buns**

1 **cup lightly packed arugula or spinach leaves**

Serving suggestion:

Grilled Eggplant Salad (page 79) or Grilled Antipasto Skewers (page 69) makes a perfect side for these Italian-style burgers.

herbed tenderloin steaks & vegetables

A bouquet of herbs, beautiful tomatoes, and asparagus lends fresh-from-the-garden flavor to this meat-and-vegetables meal. Stir purchased roasted garlic into deli mashed potatoes and serve up French bread to complete a patio-perfect repast.

2 cloves garlic

¼ cup loosely packed fresh basil leaves

2 tablespoons fresh thyme leaves

1 tablespoon fresh rosemary

1 tablespoon fresh mint leaves

2 tablespoons olive oil

½ teaspoon salt

½ teaspoon pepper

4 beef tenderloin steaks, cut 1 inch thick (about 1 pound)

2 large yellow tomatoes, halved crosswise

1 pound asparagus spears, trimmed

Serving suggestion:

For dessert, try Bananas Suzette over Grilled Pound Cake (page 87).

Prep: 15 minutes   Grill: 8 minutes   Makes 4 servings

With food processor or blender running, add garlic through feed tube or lid. Process or blend until garlic is finely chopped. Add basil, thyme, rosemary, and mint. Cover and process or blend until herbs are chopped. With food processor or blender running, add oil in a thin, steady stream. (When necessary, stop food processor or blender and use a rubber scraper to scrape the sides of bowl or container.) Stir in salt and pepper.

Spread some of the herb mixture evenly over both sides of the steaks and over cut sides of tomatoes; set aside. Fold 18×12-inch piece of heavy foil in half to make a double thickness of foil that measures 9×12 inches. Place asparagus in the center of the foil. Add remaining herb mixture, turning asparagus to coat evenly. Grill steaks and asparagus (on foil) on the rack of an uncovered grill directly over medium heat for 5 minutes. Turn steaks and asparagus spears; add tomatoes to grill. Grill until steaks are desired doneness. (Allow 3 to 7 minutes more for medium-rare and 7 to 10 minutes more for medium doneness.) Grill vegetables until asparagus is crisp-tender and tomatoes are hot (do not turn).

Nutrition facts per serving: 245 cal., 14 g total fat (4 g sat. fat), 65 mg chol., 322 mg sodium, 6 g carbo., 2 g fiber, 24 g pro. Daily values: 8% vit. A, 47% vit. C, 3% calcium, 3% iron

flank steak on tap

Hearty pub food like this beer-marinated beef steak is back in style for good reason—it's warm and welcoming. On a cool fall evening, enjoy it outdoors with the seasonal colors, an Oktoberfest brew, and, of course, lots of good conversation.

**Prep: 20 minutes   Marinate: 4 to 24 hours
Grill: 12 minutes   Makes 4 servings**

For marinade, in a small saucepan combine onion, beer, Worcestershire sauce, brown sugar, garlic, bay leaf, and the ¼ teaspoon pepper. Bring to boiling; reduce heat. Simmer, uncovered, for 4 to 5 minutes or until sugar is dissolved and onion and garlic are beginning to soften. Cool to room temperature. Diagonally score both sides of the steak at 1-inch intervals, making a diamond pattern. Place the steak in a plastic bag set in a shallow dish. Pour marinade over steak; close bag. Marinate in refrigerator for at least 4 hours or up to 24 hours, turning occasionally.

Drain steak, reserving marinade. Remove bay leaf. Season steak with salt. Grill on rack of an uncovered grill directly over medium heat to desired doneness, turning once. (Allow 12 to 14 minutes for medium doneness.) Meanwhile, for sauce, in a small saucepan combine reserved marinade and cornstarch. Cook and stir over medium heat until the sauce is thickened and bubbly. Cook and stir 2 minutes more. To serve, cut steak across the grain into ⅛- to ¼-inch-thick slices; spoon sauce over steak. If desired, sprinkle with parsley and additional pepper.

Nutrition facts per serving: 185 cal., 7 g total fat (3 g sat. fat), 44 mg chol., 221 mg sodium, 10 g carbo., 1 g fiber, 17 g pro. Daily values: 0% vit. A, 25% vit. C, 2% calcium, 16% iron

1   large onion, thinly sliced

¾   cup beer

3   tablespoons Worcestershire sauce

2   tablespoons brown sugar

3   cloves garlic, minced

1   bay leaf

¼   teaspoon coarsely ground pepper

1   1¼- to 1½-pound beef flank steak

¼   teaspoon salt

2   teaspoons cornstarch

     Snipped fresh parsley (optional)

     Coarsely ground pepper (optional)

Serving suggestion:

Add steamed green beans and mashed potatoes and dinner's done!

veal chops with pesto-stuffed mushrooms

Short on time tonight? Briefly soak tender veal chops in a white wine-sage marinade and toss them on the grill. Short on time tomorrow? Marinate the meat overnight for a dinner in no time and for more flavorful chops, too (pictured on cover).

14

4 veal loin chops, cut ¾ inch
   thick (about 1¼ pounds)

¼ cup dry white wine

3 large cloves garlic, minced

1 tablespoon snipped
   fresh sage or thyme

1 tablespoon white wine
   Worcestershire sauce

1 tablespoon olive oil

8 large fresh mushrooms
   (2 to 2½ inches in diameter)

2 to 3 tablespoons prepared pesto

Serving suggestion:

Slender steamed baby carrots and hot cooked rice round out this meal.

Prep: 10 minutes   Marinate: 15 minutes to 24 hours
Grill: 12 minutes   Makes 4 servings

For marinade, combine wine, garlic, herb, Worcestershire sauce, and oil. Place veal chops in a large plastic bag set in a shallow dish. Pour over chops; close bag. Marinate at room temperature for 15 minutes. (Or, marinate in refrigerator for up to 24 hours, turning bag occasionally.)

Drain veal chops, reserving marinade. Sprinkle chops with freshly ground black pepper. Grill chops on the rack of an uncovered grill directly over medium heat to desired doneness, turning and brushing with marinade halfway through cooking. (Allow 12 to 14 minutes for medium-rare and 15 to 17 minutes for medium doneness.)

Meanwhile, carefully remove stems from mushrooms; chop stems for another use or discard. Brush mushroom caps with reserved marinade; place mushrooms, stem sides down, on grill rack. Grill for 4 minutes. Turn stem sides up; spoon some pesto into each. Grill about 4 minutes more or until heated through. Serve mushrooms with veal chops.

Nutrition facts per serving: 285 cal., 16 g total fat (2 g sat. fat), 100 mg chol., 157 mg sodium, 4 g carbo., 1 g fiber, 28 g pro. Daily values: 0% vit. A, 3% vit. C, 3% calcium, 9% iron

mesquite mixed grill

Can't decide between pork chops and sausage? Have both! The sweet smoke of mesquite infuses this mixed grill with an unmistakably good flavor. A sauce made with mustard (try any whole-grain variety that suits you) makes a stylish condiment.

2 cups mesquite wood chips

4 boneless pork top loin chops, cut ¾ inch thick (about 1 pound)

4 small leeks or 1 medium red sweet pepper, seeded and cut into 1-inch pieces

⅛ teaspoon garlic salt

¼ teaspoon black pepper

8 ounces fully cooked turkey Polish sausage, cut into 4 equal portions

⅓ cup whole-grain mustard

2 teaspoons white wine vinegar or cider vinegar

1 teaspoon snipped fresh tarragon

Serving suggestion:

Serve this hearty meat mixture with grilled garlic bread.

Prep: 10 minutes   Grill: 9 minutes   Makes 4 servings

At least 1 hour before grilling, soak wood chips in enough water to cover. Trim fat from pork chops. If using leeks, rinse well, trim root end, and cut 3 to 4 inches off each top and discard. Sprinkle garlic salt and black pepper evenly over chops and leeks or sweet pepper.

Drain wood chips. In a grill with a cover arrange preheated coals in even layer. Sprinkle wood chips onto coals. Place the chops and leeks or sweet pepper on grill rack directly over medium coals; cover grill and cook for 5 minutes. Turn chops; add the sausage to grill. Cover and grill 4 to 6 minutes more or until the chops are slightly pink in center and juices run clear, turning sausage once.

Meanwhile, combine mustard, vinegar, and tarragon. Serve as a dipping sauce with chops, sausages, and leeks or sweet pepper.

Nutrition facts per serving: 282 cal., 12 g total fat (3 g sat. fat), 86 mg chol., 880 mg sodium, 12 g carbo., 4 g fiber, 27 g pro. Daily values: 0% vit. A, 29% vit. C, 7% calcium, 19% iron

smoke 'em
Tossing wood chips on your grill gives foods a wood-smoked aroma and flavor. Generally, wood chips need to be soaked in enough water to cover them for about an hour. Afterwards drain the wood chips well and toss onto hot coals. Good choices for wood chips include mesquite, alder, hickory, oak, and sweetish fruitwoods such as apple, cherry, and peach.

pork chops with savory mushroom stuffing

There's a surprise inside the pocket of these quick-cooking boneless pork chops—a mouthwatering mushroom stuffing. Instead of white button mushrooms, try using brown crimini mushrooms for even more mushroom flavor.

Prep: 15 minutes   Grill: 20 minutes   Makes 4 servings

For stuffing, in a large skillet heat oil over medium heat. Add green onion and cook for 1 minute. Stir in mushrooms, rosemary, salt, and pepper. Cook and stir 2 to 3 minutes more or until mushrooms are tender. Remove from heat.

Trim fat from chops. Make a pocket in each chop by cutting from fat side almost to, but not through, the opposite side. Spoon stuffing into pockets in chops. If necessary, secure with wooden toothpicks.

Brush chops with Worcestershire sauce. Season chops lightly with additional salt and pepper. Grill chops on the rack of an uncovered grill directly over medium heat about 20 minutes or until juices run clear, turning once. To serve, remove wooden toothpicks.

Nutrition facts per serving: 241 cal., 14 g total fat (4 g sat. fat), 77 mg chol., 218 mg sodium, 4 g carbo., 1 g fiber, 25 g pro. Daily values: 1% vit. A, 13% vit. C, 1% calcium, 14% iron

2 teaspoons olive oil

2 tablespoons thinly sliced green onions

1 8-ounce package fresh mushrooms, coarsely chopped

2 teaspoons snipped fresh rosemary or oregano

⅛ teaspoon salt

⅛ teaspoon pepper

4 boneless pork loin chops, cut 1 inch thick

2 teaspoons Worcestershire sauce

Serving suggestion:

Pair these pork chops with Warm Asparagus, Fennel, & Spinach Salad (page 73).

grilled italian sausage with sweet & sour peppers

Sicilians love sweet and sour flavors and toss super-sweet raisins into their delicious meat and fish dishes with culinary abandon. Here, grilled Italian sausage is presented on a bed of piquant, sweet grilled vegetables.

19

Prep: 20 minutes   Grill: 10 minutes   Makes 6 servings

In a small nonstick skillet cook and stir almonds for 1 to 2 minutes or until golden brown. Stir in raisins. Remove skillet from heat. Let stand for 1 minute. Carefully stir in vinegar, sugar, salt, and pepper. Return to heat; cook and stir just until the sugar dissolves.

Drizzle oil over sweet pepper strips and onion slices. Prick sausages several times with a fork. Grill vegetables and sausages on the rack of an uncovered grill directly over medium heat for 10 to 15 minutes or until no pink remains in the sausages and vegetables are tender, turning once.

In the large bowl toss the vegetables with the almond mixture; spoon onto a serving platter. Place sausages atop.

Nutrition facts per serving: 276 cal., 19 g total fat (6 g sat. fat), 59 mg chol., 604 mg sodium, 15 g carbo., 1 g fiber, 13 g pro. Daily values: 19% vit. A, 102% vit. C, 2% calcium, 9% iron

3 **tablespoons slivered almonds**

¼ **cup raisins**

3 **tablespoons red wine vinegar**

2 **tablespoons sugar**

¼ **teaspoon salt**

⅛ **teaspoon black pepper**

1 **tablespoon olive oil**

2 **green sweet peppers, cut into 1-inch-wide strips**

2 **red sweet peppers, cut into 1-inch-wide strips**

1 **medium red onion, thickly sliced**

6 **sweet Italian sausage links**

Serving suggestion:

For more Italian goodness, grill purchased polenta alongside the sausages and vegetables.

grilled mustard-glazed pork

This express-lane dinner gives you time to slow down as soon as you walk in the door. Simply mix up the marinade and pour it over the pork. Let it sit in the refrigerator while you unwind. Grill about 20 minutes and dinner's done!

 2 **12- to 14-ounce pork tenderloins**
 ½ **cup apple juice**
 ¼ **cup cider vinegar**
 2 **large shallots, minced**
 ¼ **cup coarse-grain brown mustard**
 2 **tablespoons olive oil**
 1 **tablespoon brown sugar**
 1½ **teaspoons soy sauce**
    Dash pepper
    Snipped fresh chives (optional)

Serving suggestion:

Try serving these sweet and savory pork tenderloins with Apple & Grilled Chicken Salad (page 38), minus the chicken.

Prep: 10 minutes   Marinate: 30 minutes
Grill: 23 minutes   Makes 6 servings

Trim fat from tenderloins. Place tenderloins in a plastic bag set in a shallow dish. For marinade, combine apple juice, vinegar, shallots, mustard, oil, brown sugar, soy sauce, and pepper. Pour over meat; close bag. Marinate in refrigerator for 30 minutes, turning bag occasionally.

In a grill with a cover arrange preheated coals around a drip pan. Drain tenderloins, reserving marinade. Place tenderloins on the grill rack directly over medium-hot coals; grill for 8 minutes, turning once to brown both sides. Move tenderloins over drip pan; insert meat thermometer in center of thickest tenderloin. Cover and grill for 15 to 20 minutes more or until meat thermometer registers 160°.

Meanwhile, for sauce, pour reserved marinade into a medium saucepan. Bring to boiling and reduce heat. Simmer, uncovered, about 8 minutes or until reduced to ⅔ cup. Slice the tenderloins across the grain. Serve with the sauce. If desired, sprinkle with chives.

Nutrition facts per serving: 215 cal., 9 g total fat (2 g sat. fat), 81 mg chol., 280 mg sodium, 7 g carbo., 0 g fiber, 26 g pro. Daily values: 8% vit. A, 1% vit. C, 2% calcium, 12% iron

fennel & pork sausage
with grape relish

Two kinds of fennel give great flavor to these spirited sausage patties. Aromatic fennel seed lends the patties its essence, and alongside the patties, crisp fresh fennel cooks with balsamic vinegar and red grapes to make an elegant sauce.

Prep: 15 minutes   Grill: 14 minutes   Makes 4 servings

In a large bowl combine the egg and, if desired, bourbon. Stir in rolled oats, fennel seed, garlic, lemon peel, paprika, ½ teaspoon salt, and ½ teaspoon pepper. Add ground pork. Mix well. Shape the pork mixture into four ¾-inch-thick patties. Set aside.

Fold a 36×18-inch piece of heavy foil in half to make a double thickness of foil that measures 18×18 inches. Place the grapes, chopped fennel, margarine, and vinegar in the center of the foil. Sprinkle with additional salt and pepper. Bring up 2 opposite edges of foil and seal with a double fold. Fold remaining edges to completely enclose the grape mixture, leaving space for steam to build.

Grill the pork patties and the grape mixture on the rack of an uncovered grill directly over medium heat for 14 to 16 minutes or until no pink remains in the patties, turning once. To serve, spoon grape mixture over the grilled patties. Sprinkle with the fresh parsley.

Nutrition facts per serving: 284 cal., 14 g total fat (5 g sat. fat), 106 mg chol., 409 mg sodium, 23 g carbo., 7 g fiber, 18 g pro. Daily values: 11% vit. A, 28% vit. C, 5% calcium, 17% iron

- 1 **slightly beaten egg**
- 1 **tablespoon bourbon (optional)**
- ½ **cup quick-cooking rolled oats**
- 1 **tablespoon fennel seed, crushed**
- 1 **large clove garlic, minced**
- 1 **teaspoon finely shredded lemon peel**
- 1 **teaspoon paprika**
- 1 **pound lean ground pork**
- 1½ **cups red seedless grapes, halved**
- 1 **small fennel bulb, coarsely chopped (1 cup)**
- 1 **tablespoon margarine or butter**
- 2 **tablespoons balsamic vinegar**
- ¼ **cup snipped fresh parsley**

Serving suggestion:

Hot buttered orzo is a simple side for these homemade sausage patties with grape sauce.

jamaican pork kabobs

Jamaican doesn't always mean jerk. These pork and vegetable kabobs get an island air from mango chutney and a liberal dose of Pickapeppa sauce, a much milder version of its famous relative, Tabasco. Cool the fire with slices of mango and lime.

2   ears of corn, husked
       and cleaned

1   12- to 14-ounce pork tenderloin

1   small red onion, cut into
       ½-inch-thick wedges

16 baby pattypan squash,
       about 1 inch in diameter,
       or 4 tomatillos, quartered

¼   cup mango chutney, finely chopped

3   tablespoons Pickapeppa sauce

1   tablespoon cooking oil

1   tablespoon water

Serving suggestion:

Present these kabobs on a bed of hot cooked rice, and follow up with Grilled Fruit Kabobs with Lime-Yogurt Sauce (page 84).

Prep: 15 minutes   Grill: 12 minutes   Makes 4 servings

Cut corn crosswise into 1-inch pieces. In medium saucepan cook corn pieces in small amount of boiling water for 3 minutes; drain and rinse with cold water. Meanwhile, cut tenderloin into 1-inch-thick slices. For kabobs, on long metal skewers alternately thread tenderloin, onion, squash or tomatillos, and corn.

In small bowl combine chutney, Pickapeppa sauce, oil, and water; set aside. Grill kabobs on the rack of an uncovered grill directly over medium heat for 12 to 14 minutes or until no pink remains in the pork and the vegetables are tender, turning once and brushing with the chutney mixture during the last 5 minutes of grilling.

Nutrition facts per serving: 252 cal., 7 g total fat (2 g sat. fat), 60 mg chol., 127 mg sodium, 27 g carbo., 3 g fiber, 21 g pro. Daily values: 3% vit. A, 13% vit. C, 2% calcium, 10% iron

summer supper **sippers**

Warm summer evenings call for cooling drinks. Consider these:

- Sparkling water with fruit-juice cubes (orange, cranberry, mango, or papaya juice frozen in ice cube trays) and fresh mint.
- Spritzers made with sparkling water, cranberry juice, and a lime twist.
- Special iced teas, made with brewed green, herbal, or raspberry- or currant-flavored black tea.

grilled lamb chops
with **mint** marinade

Petite lamb chops are pretty on their own—what's even more attractive about these chops is that they can marinate in the refrigerator overnight and are ready to eat after about 10 minutes of grilling. Serve them with wedges of fresh lemon.

8 **well-trimmed lamb loin chops, cut 1 inch thick (about 2 pounds)**

2 **tablespoons lemon juice**

2 **tablespoons olive oil**

3 **cloves garlic, minced**

¼ **cup snipped fresh mint**

¼ **teaspoon pepper**

¼ **teaspoon salt**

Serving suggestion:

Jasmine-Mint Tea Rice with Peas (page 71) is the perfect foil for these tender chops.

Prep: 10 minutes   Marinate: 30 minutes to 24 hours
Grill: 10 minutes   Makes 4 servings

Trim fat from chops. Place chops in a plastic bag set in a shallow dish. For marinade, combine lemon juice, oil, garlic, 3 tablespoons of the mint, and the pepper. Pour over the chops; close bag. Marinate in the refrigerator for at least 30 minutes or up to 24 hours. Drain chops, discarding marinade. Sprinkle chops with the salt.

Grill chops on rack of an uncovered grill directly over medium heat to desired doneness, turning once. (Allow 10 to 14 minutes for medium-rare and 14 to 16 minutes for medium doneness.) Sprinkle with remaining mint.

Nutrition facts per serving: 310 cal., 18 g total fat (5 g sat. fat), 107 mg chol., 229 mg sodium, 2 g carbo., 0 g fiber, 34 g pro. Daily values: 1% vit. A, 12% vit. C, 2% calcium, 21% iron

make mine **marinated**

A good soak is good for the soul—and it's good for your food, too. Marinating is great in two ways: it adds flavor and it tenderizes meats. Generally marinades are made with an acidic liquid (which has the tenderizing effect) such as wine, vinegar, or citrus juice, plus herbs and seasonings—and sometimes a little oil. The longer the meat spends luxuriating in the liquid, the more great flavor it will have.

grilled greek leg of lamb

Leg of lamb in less than an hour? You bet, if it's sliced thin and flash-grilled after a quick soak in a lemon-oregano marinade. A sauce of grilled tomatoes mixed with cinnamon, feta cheese, and Greek olives adds an authentic taste of the islands.

Prep: 20 minutes   Marinate: 20 minutes to 24 hours
Grill: 8 minutes   Makes 6 servings

Slice lamb across grain into ½- to ¾-inch-thick pieces; place in a large bowl. For marinade, stir together the lemon peel, half of the lemon juice, 4 tablespoons of the oil, the oregano, ½ teaspoon salt, and ⅛ teaspoon pepper. Cover and marinate at room temperature for 20 minutes. (Or, place lamb in a plastic bag set in a shallow dish. Pour marinade over lamb; close bag. Marinate in the refrigerator for at least 8 hours or up to 24 hours, turning bag occasionally.) In a large bowl combine remaining lemon juice, olives, 1 tablespoon of the remaining oil, the parsley, feta cheese, cinnamon, and ¼ teaspoon pepper; set aside.

Drain lamb, discard marinade. Brush tomatoes with the remaining 1 tablespoon oil. Grill lamb and tomatoes on the rack of an uncovered grill directly over medium-hot heat for 8 to 10 minutes or until lamb is desired doneness and tomatoes are slightly charred, turning once. Transfer tomatoes to cutting board; cool slightly and slice. Toss the tomatoes with the feta cheese mixture; serve with lamb.

Nutrition facts per serving: 256 cal., 14 g total fat (4 g sat. fat), 66 mg chol., 493 mg sodium,
11 g carbo., 0 g fiber, 22 g pro. Daily values: 15% vit. A, 80% vit. C, 6% calcium, 18% iron

1½ to 2 pounds boneless
    leg of lamb, trimmed

1 tablespoon finely shredded
    lemon peel

⅔ cup lemon juice

6 tablespoons olive oil

⅓ cup snipped fresh oregano

¼ cup pitted, sliced kalamata olives

½ cup snipped fresh parsley

½ cup crumbled feta cheese

¼ teaspoon ground cinnamon

2 pounds plum tomatoes

Serving suggestion:

While the lamb is grilling, cook some couscous to soak up the sauce from the fresh tomatoes.

tandoori-style lamb chops

You don't need the traditional Indian brick-and-clay oven called a tandoor to make these chops, but the delicious characteristic of tandoori cuisine—quick cooking to seal in juices and flavors—is present in these Indian-spiced lamb chops.

Prep: 20 minutes   Grill: 10 minutes   Makes 4 servings

In small bowl combine oil, garlic, ginger, garam masala, and ½ teaspoon salt. Brush onto all sides of the chops and squash.

Grill chops and squash on the rack of an uncovered grill directly over medium heat to desired doneness and until squash is tender, turning once. (Allow 10 to 14 minutes for medium-rare doneness.) For the last 2 minutes of grilling, place pita rounds on grill rack to heat.

Meanwhile, in a small bowl combine yogurt and mint. Transfer vegetables to a cutting board; cool slightly and slice diagonally ½ inch thick. Serve squash, pita bread, and chutney with chops.

Nutrition facts per serving: 615 cal., 22 g total fat (6 g sat. fat), 135 mg chol., 735 mg sodium, 51 g carbo., 1 g fiber, 51 g pro. Daily values: 3% vit. A, 11% vit. C, 14% calcium, 40% iron

Note: For homemade garam masala, combine 1 teaspoon ground cumin, 1 teaspoon ground coriander, ½ teaspoon pepper, ½ teaspoon ground cardamom, ¼ teaspoon ground cinnamon, and ¼ teaspoon ground cloves.

2 tablespoons cooking oil

6 cloves garlic, minced

2 teaspoons grated fresh ginger

1 tablespoon garam masala*

8 well-trimmed lamb loin chops, cut 1 inch thick (about 2 pounds)

2 medium yellow summer squash and/or zucchini, halved lengthwise

4 pita bread rounds

½ cup plain low-fat yogurt

1 tablespoon snipped fresh mint

¼ cup chutney or hot chutney

Serving suggestion:

Start out this meal with papdum, crisp black-pepper and lentil crackers, found at Indian markets.

the
perfect bird

grilled **vietnamese** chicken breasts

This is no ho-hum chicken sandwich. Spicy-sweet peanut sauce and crisp broccoli slaw lend an Asian accent to this out-of-the-ordinary grilled chicken.

Prep: 15 minutes   Grill: 12 minutes   Makes 4 servings

Rinse chicken; pat dry. Combine sesame oil and crushed red pepper; brush over chicken.

Grill chicken on the lightly greased rack of an uncovered grill directly over medium heat for 12 to 15 minutes or until tender and no longer pink, turning once.

Meanwhile, for sauce, in a small saucepan,* stir together sugar, peanut butter, soy sauce, oil, garlic, and 2 tablespoons water. Heat on grill rack until sugar is dissolved, stirring frequently. For the last 1 minute of grilling, place split rolls on the grill rack to toast.

To serve, place cooked chicken breasts on bottom halves of rolls; spoon on sauce and top with radish sprouts, broccoli, peanuts (if desired), and roll tops.

Nutrition facts per serving: 360 cal., 14 g total fat (3 g sat. fat), 59 mg chol., 852 mg sodium, 29 g carbo., 1 g fiber, 28 g pro. Daily values: 3% vit. A, 14% vit. C, 4% calcium, 14% iron

*Note: The heat from the grill will blacken the outside of the saucepan, so use an old one or a small cast-iron skillet.

- **4 medium skinless, boneless chicken breast halves (about 1 pound total)**
- **2 teaspoons toasted sesame oil**
- **½ teaspoon crushed red pepper**
- **2 tablespoons sugar**
- **2 tablespoons peanut butter**
- **2 tablespoons soy sauce**
- **1 tablespoon cooking oil**
- **1 clove garlic, minced**
- **4 French-style rolls, split**
- **¼ cup radish sprouts**
- **½ cup packaged shredded broccoli (broccoli slaw mix)**
- **¼ cup chopped peanuts (optional)**

Serving suggestion:

Serve these sandwiches with a homemade Asian-style salad of paper-thin-sliced cucumber dressed with a bottled sesame vinaigrette.

curried chicken
& potato packets

Unwrap a little fun tonight! You'll curry favor from your family with the Indian flavors of chicken and vegetables cooked in a velvety sour cream sauce. Individual serving packets give this dish flair—precooked chicken strips make it fast.

1 9-ounce package frozen cooked chicken breast strips

4 medium potatoes, cut into ¾-inch cubes

1½ cups packaged peeled baby carrots

1 small onion, thinly sliced

½ cup dairy sour cream or plain low-fat yogurt

1 teaspoon curry powder

1 teaspoon Dijon-style mustard

½ teaspoon salt

½ teaspoon paprika

⅛ teaspoon crushed red pepper

Serving suggestion:

Something spicy calls for something sweet. Try Honey-Glazed Bananas (page 74) as a side.

Prep: 10 minutes   Grill: 25 minutes   Makes 4 servings

Tear off four 24×18-inch pieces of heavy foil. Fold each piece in half to make a double thickness of foil that measures 12×18 inches; set aside.

In a large bowl combine frozen chicken, potatoes, carrots, and onion; set aside. In a small bowl combine sour cream, curry powder, mustard, salt, paprika, and crushed red pepper. Pour over chicken mixture; toss gently.

Divide mixture among the foil pieces. Bring up opposite long edges of a foil piece and seal with a double fold. Fold ends to completely enclose chicken mixture, leaving space for steam to build. Repeat with remaining pieces of foil.

Grill the chicken mixture on the rack of an uncovered grill directly over medium heat about 25 minutes or until vegetables are tender.

Nutrition facts per serving: 371 cal., 11 g total fat (5 g sat. fat), 70 mg chol., 414 mg sodium, 44 g carbo., 3 g fiber, 24 g pro. Daily values: 129% vit. A, 41% vit. C, 6% calcium, 21% iron

grilled asian chicken & noodles

Keep a cool noodle with this quick-to-fix dish. Cold udon noodles flavored with sesame-ginger dressing are tossed with crisp cabbage, warm chicken, and eggplant. Look for udon—a thick Japanese noodle similar to spaghetti—at Asian markets.

Prep: 20 minutes   Grill: 12 minutes
Cool: 5 minutes   Makes 4 servings

Cook noodles according to package directions. Meanwhile, combine soy sauce, sesame oil, vinegar, garlic, ginger, and crushed red pepper. Set 2 tablespoons of the soy sauce mixture aside. Drain noodles. In a large bowl toss noodles with the remaining soy sauce mixture. Place noodle mixture in freezer to quick chill.

Rinse chicken; pat dry. Grill chicken on the lightly greased rack of an uncovered grill directly over medium heat for 12 to 15 minutes or until chicken is tender and no longer pink, turning once and brushing occasionally with the reserved soy sauce mixture. For the last 8 minutes of grilling, place eggplant slices on the rack alongside the chicken; turn once and brush occasionally with reserved soy sauce mixture. Transfer chicken and eggplant to cutting board; cool for 5 minutes and cut into cubes.

Toss chicken, eggplant, and cabbage with noodles. Sprinkle with cashews (if desired) and cilantro.

Nutrition facts per serving: 442 cal., 12 g total fat (2 g sat. fat), 108 mg chol., 646 mg sodium, 51 g carbo., 6 g fiber, 32 g pro. Daily values: 81% vit. A, 60% vit. C, 6% calcium, 28% iron

8 **ounces udon or Chinese curly noodles**

¼ **cup light soy sauce**

2 **tablespoons toasted sesame oil**

2 **tablespoons rice vinegar**

4 **cloves garlic, minced**

1½ **teaspoons grated fresh ginger**

¼ **teaspoon crushed red pepper**

4 **medium skinless, boneless chicken breast halves (about 1 pound total)**

1 **small eggplant, sliced**

4 **cups packaged shredded cabbage with carrot (coleslaw mix)**

¼ **cup chopped cashews (optional)**

2 **to 3 tablespoons chopped fresh cilantro**

Serving suggestion:

A simple and light dessert, such as chocolate-dipped fortune cookies and fruit sorbet, makes a refreshing finish to this meal.

smoky chicken wraps

It's easy to get a grip on dinner when it's mesquite-smoked chicken all wrapped up in a tomato tortilla that's slathered with tomato-and-pine nut cream cheese. For variety, try other flavored tortillas, such as spinach. Plain works, too.

Prep: 20 minutes   Marinate: 15 minutes
Grill: 10 minutes   Makes 4 servings

At least 1 hour before grilling, soak wood chips in enough water to cover. Rinse chicken; pat dry. Place chicken in a shallow dish. For marinade, combine oil, Worcestershire sauce, thyme, and ¼ teaspoon pepper; pour over chicken. Cover; marinate at room temperature for 15 minutes.

In small bowl stir together cream cheese, dried tomatoes, and nuts (if desired). If necessary, stir in enough water to make of spreading consistency. Season to taste with salt and pepper; set aside. Wrap tortillas in heavy foil.

Drain wood chips. In a grill with a cover arrange preheated coals in an even layer. Sprinkle wood chips over coals. Place chicken on a lightly greased grill rack directly over medium-hot coals. Cover and grill 10 to 12 minutes or until chicken is tender and no longer pink, turning chicken and adding tortillas halfway through grilling.

Transfer chicken breasts to a cutting board; cool slightly and thinly slice. Spread the cream cheese mixture over tortillas; sprinkle with basil. Divide chicken among tortillas; roll up.

Nutrition facts per serving: 454 cal., 21 g total fat (6 g sat. fat), 77 mg chol., 798 mg sodium, 42 g carbo., 1 g fiber, 26 g pro. Daily values: 5% vit. A, 17% vit. C, 7% calcium, 21% iron

- 2 **cups mesquite wood chips**
- 12 **ounces skinless, boneless chicken breast halves**
- 1 **tablespoon cooking oil**
- 1 **tablespoon Worcestershire sauce**
- 1 **teaspoon snipped fresh thyme**
- ½ **of an 8-ounce tub plain cream cheese**
- 2 **oil-packed dried tomatoes, drained and finely chopped**
- 2 **tablespoons chopped pine nuts or almonds (optional)**
- 4 **8- or 9-inch tomato tortillas or plain flour tortillas**
- 16 **fresh basil leaves, cut into strips**

Serving suggestion:

Toss together a simple salad of yellow or red pear tomatoes dressed with an herb vinaigrette to complete the meal.

southwest chicken salad

Grilling lends sweet oranges a pleasing smoky flavor in this refreshingly different chicken salad. To make a side salad to serve with your favorite grilled meats, poultry, or fish, simply omit the chicken.

½ cup bottled poppy seed
   salad dressing

1 small jalapeño pepper, seeded
   and finely chopped

½ teaspoon finely shredded
   orange peel

4 medium skinless, boneless
   chicken breast halves
   (about 1 pound total)

2 oranges, peeled and sliced
   ½ inch thick

1 red sweet pepper, seeded
   and quartered

8 cups torn mixed greens

1 small jicama, peeled and sliced
   into thin bite-size strips

Serving suggestion:

*A side for this main-dish salad
is as simple as a stack of warmed
flour tortillas.*

Prep: 15 minutes   Grill: 12 minutes   Makes 4 servings

In a small bowl combine dressing, jalapeño, and orange peel. Reserve all but 1 tablespoon dressing mixture. Rinse chicken; pat dry. Brush the chicken, orange slices, and sweet pepper with the 1 tablespoon dressing mixture. Grill the chicken, orange slices, and sweet pepper on the lightly greased rack of an uncovered grill directly over medium heat for 12 to 15 minutes or until chicken is tender and no longer pink, turning once. Transfer the chicken, orange slices, and sweet pepper to a cutting board; cool slightly. Cut chicken and sweet pepper into bite-size strips; quarter the orange slices.

Meanwhile, in a large salad bowl toss together the greens and jicama. Add the chicken, oranges, and sweet pepper to the salad bowl; drizzle with the reserved dressing mixture. Season to taste with black pepper.

Nutrition facts per serving: 339 cal., 18 g total fat (3 g sat. fat), 59 mg chol., 194 mg sodium, 22 g carbo., 3 g fiber, 24 g pro. Daily values: 26% vit. A, 147% vit. C, 5% calcium, 11% iron

provençal grilled chicken & herbed penne

Fresh grilled vegetables, fruity and fragrant olive oil, a very French blend of herbs, and fresh thyme that grows in abundance on the rocky hillsides of the south of France give this dish the flavor of Provence. Enjoy it with a glass of chilled white wine.

Start to finish: 25 minutes   Makes 4 servings

Cook pasta according to package directions. Meanwhile, rinse chicken; pat dry. Brush chicken, zucchini, and asparagus with 1 tablespoon of the oil; sprinkle all sides with fines herbes and ½ teaspoon salt.

Place the chicken in center of the lightly greased rack of an uncovered grill; place the zucchini and asparagus around chicken. Grill directly over medium heat for 12 to 15 minutes or until chicken is tender and no longer pink and vegetables are tender, turning once.

Transfer chicken and vegetables to cutting board; cool slightly. Cut chicken and zucchini into 1-inch cubes; slice asparagus into 1-inch-long pieces. Drain pasta; return to saucepan. Add chicken, vegetables, remaining oil, and thyme to pasta; toss well. Divide among 4 dinner plates; top with cheese and season with pepper.

Nutrition facts per serving: 480 cal., 17 g total fat (2 g sat. fat), 69 mg chol., 492 mg sodium, 45 g carbo., 4 g fiber, 35 g pro. Daily values: 7% vit. A, 20% vit. C, 15% calcium, 17% iron

culinary **cousins**
Fines herbs and herbes de Provence—both French herb blends—are interchangeable. Fines herbs is a quartet of chervil, chives, parsley, and tarragon. Herbes de Provence is a melange of basil, fennel, lavender, marjoram, rosemary, sage, savory, and thyme.

8 ounces dried tomato or garlic and herb-flavored penne pasta or plain penne pasta

4 medium skinless, boneless chicken breast halves (about 1 pound total)

1 medium zucchini, halved lengthwise

8 thick asparagus spears (8 to 10 ounces total), trimmed

3 tablespoons olive oil

1 tablespoon fines herbes or herbes de Provence, crushed

1 tablespoon snipped fresh thyme

½ cup finely shredded Asiago or Pecorino Romano cheese

Serving suggestion:

All this pasta dish needs is a crisp romaine or mesclun salad and some crusty French rolls.

sesame-ginger barbecued chicken

This Asian-style barbecue sauce spiked with Oriental chili sauce is so good, you'll definitely want to warm up the extra and pass it at the table with the chicken. But watch closely—or the bowl may be empty by the time it gets to you!

⅓ cup plum sauce or sweet-sour sauce

¼ cup water

3 tablespoons hoisin sauce

1½ teaspoons sesame seed
(toasted, if desired)

1 clove garlic, minced

1 teaspoon grated fresh ginger
or ¼ teaspoon ground ginger

¼ to ½ teaspoon Oriental chili
sauce or several dashes bottled
hot pepper sauce

6 small skinless, boneless chicken
breast halves and/or thighs
(about 1½ pounds total)

Serving suggestion:

Besides the extra sauce, serve this sweet-savory barbecued chicken with bottled sesame-vinaigrette dressed slaw—and Grilled Pineapple with Sugared Wontons (page 89) for dessert.

Prep: 10 minutes   Grill: 12 minutes   Makes 6 servings

For sauce, in a small saucepan combine all of the ingredients except the chicken. Bring to boiling over medium heat, stirring frequently; reduce heat. Simmer, covered, for 3 minutes. Set aside.

Rinse chicken; pat dry. Grill chicken on the lightly greased rack of an uncovered grill directly over medium heat for 12 to 15 minutes or until tender and no longer pink, turning once and brushing with sauce once or twice during the last 5 minutes of grilling.

In a small saucepan heat the remaining sauce until bubbly; pass with chicken.

Nutrition facts per serving: 166 cal., 4 g total fat (1 g sat. fat), 59 mg chol., 216 mg sodium, 9 g carbo., 0 g fiber, 22 g pro. Daily values: 1% vit. A, 1% vit. C, 1% calcium, 5% iron

it's **hot, hot, hot** (or not)
Here's a simple way to test the approximate temperature of your coals. Hold your hand over where the food will cook for as long as it is comfortable. The number of seconds you can hold it there gives you a clue.

Number of seconds	Coal Temperature
2	High
3	Medium-high
4	Medium
5	Medium-low
6	Low

apple & grilled chicken salad

Pick your favorite apples to make this salad. Either red or green apples work fine—just make sure they're a tart variety, such as Granny Smith, McIntosh, or Jonathan.

⅓ cup apple jelly

¼ cup horseradish mustard

12 ounces skinless, boneless chicken breast halves (about 3 medium)

4 cups mesclun or torn mixed greens

2 tart medium apples, cored and sliced

⅓ cup coarsely chopped walnuts (toasted, if desired)

1 tablespoon cider vinegar

1 tablespoon salad oil

Serving suggestion:

Warm corn muffins or corn bread is all that's needed to complete this main-dish salad meal.

Prep: 20 minutes   Grill: 12 minutes   Makes 4 servings

In a small saucepan melt apple jelly over low heat. Remove from heat; stir in mustard. Reserve all but 2 tablespoons jelly mixture. Rinse chicken; pat dry. Grill chicken on the lightly greased rack of an uncovered grill directly over medium heat for 12 to 15 minutes or until tender and no longer pink, turning once and brushing occasionally with the 2 tablespoons jelly mixture during the last 5 minutes of grilling. Transfer chicken to a cutting board; cool slightly and bias-slice.

Meanwhile, toss the mesclun with the apples and walnuts. For dressing, stir together the reserved jelly mixture, vinegar, and oil. Divide the greens mixture among 4 dinner plates. Arrange chicken atop the greens; drizzle with the dressing.

Nutrition facts per serving: 307 cal., 13 g total fat (2 g sat. fat), 45 mg chol., 186 mg sodium, 30 g carbo., 2 g fiber, 19 g pro. Daily values: 2% vit. A, 11% vit. C, 3% calcium, 10% iron

west indies chicken
with grilled fruit

Who says exotic has to be hard? This innovative, island-inspired, sweet-and-savory dish of grilled tropical fruit and chicken glossed with a spicy, herb-infused marmalade glaze is as easy as can be.

39

Prep: 15 minutes   Grill: 12 minutes   Makes 4 servings

In a small bowl combine grapefruit peel, orange marmalade, oil, thyme, coriander, paprika, and ¼ teaspoon salt; set aside.

Peel and quarter grapefruit and kiwifruit. Pit and quarter nectarines. Cut carambola into ½-inch-thick slices. Thread fruits on 4 metal skewers. Rinse chicken; pat dry. Grill chicken on the lightly greased rack of an uncovered grill directly over medium heat for 12 to 15 minutes or until chicken is tender and no longer pink, turning once. For the last 8 minutes of grilling, place fruit skewers on grill rack directly over medium heat. Brush fruit and chicken often with marmalade mixture; turn fruit once.

Nutrition facts per serving: 288 cal., 7 g total fat (1 g sat. fat), 59 mg chol., 192 mg sodium, 36 g carbo., 3 g fiber, 24 g pro. Daily values: 12% vit. A, 142% vit. C, 5% calcium, 11% iron

- **2 teaspoons finely shredded grapefruit or orange peel**
- **3 tablespoons orange marmalade**
- **2 teaspoons olive oil**
- **1 tablespoon snipped fresh thyme**
- **2½ teaspoons ground coriander**
- **½ teaspoon hot Hungarian paprika or ⅛ teaspoon ground red pepper**
- **1 small ruby red grapefruit**
- **2 ripe, yet firm, kiwifruit**
- **2 medium ripe, yet firm, nectarines**
- **2 ripe, yet firm, carambola (star fruit)**
- **4 medium skinless, boneless chicken breast halves (about 1 pound total)**

Serving suggestion:

While the chicken and fruit are grilling, cook some rice or couscous for a side dish.

stuffed turkey tenderloins

There's more than one way to stuff a turkey. Fresh spinach and tangy goat cheese make a melt-in-your-mouth filling in these turkey tenderloins. When sliced, the rosy-red, spicy crust on the meat yields to a juicy, tender interior.

Prep: 15 minutes   Grill: 16 minutes   Makes 4 servings

Rinse turkey; pat dry. Make a pocket in each tenderloin by cutting lengthwise from one side almost to, but not through, the opposite side; set aside. In a bowl combine the spinach, cheese, and black pepper. Spoon spinach mixture into pockets. Tie 100% cotton kitchen string around each tenderloin in 3 or 4 places to hold in stuffing.

In small bowl combine oil, paprika, salt, and ground red pepper; brush evenly over tenderloins. Grill on the lightly greased rack of an uncovered grill directly over medium heat for 16 to 20 minutes or until turkey is tender and no longer pink in center of the thickest part; turn once. Remove and discard strings; slice tenderloins crosswise.

Nutrition facts per serving: 220 cal., 12 g total fat (4 g sat. fat), 68 mg chol., 458 mg sodium, 1 g carbo., 1 g fiber, 26 g pro. Daily values: 24% vit. A, 14% vit. C, 5% calcium, 13% iron

- 2 **8-ounce turkey breast tenderloins**
- 2 **cups chopped fresh spinach leaves**
- 3 **ounces semisoft goat cheese (chévre) or feta cheese, crumbled (about ¾ cup)**
- ½ **teaspoon black pepper**
- 1 **tablespoon olive oil**
- 1 **teaspoon paprika**
- ½ **teaspoon salt**
- ⅛ **to ¼ teaspoon ground red pepper**

Serving suggestion:

Fix up purchased mashed potatoes with your favorite fresh herb and serve the turkey and potatoes with slices of honeydew melon.

turkey burgers with fresh curry catsup

America's favorite condiment goes haute cuisine! Plain old catsup gets a lift from fresh tomatoes, cilantro, and curry powder to dress up a burger flavored with ginger, garlic, and more curry. Lightly grilled pita bread fills in for a more ordinary bun.

42

1 **beaten egg**

¼ **cup fine dry bread crumbs**

2 **tablespoons snipped fresh cilantro**

2 **teaspoons grated fresh ginger**

1 **clove garlic, minced**

½ **teaspoon salt**

½ **teaspoon curry powder**

¼ **teaspoon freshly ground black pepper**

1 **pound ground raw turkey**

1 **recipe Curry Catsup**

2 **large pita bread rounds (optional)**

Serving suggestion:

Serve these out-of-the-ordinary burgers with sweet-potato chips— found in the snack aisle of most supermarkets.

Prep: 20 minutes Grill: 14 minutes Makes 4 servings

In a large bowl combine egg, bread crumbs, cilantro, ginger, garlic, salt, curry powder, and pepper. Add turkey and mix well. Form turkey mixture into four ¾-inch-thick patties. (If mixture is sticky, moisten hands with water.) Grill patties on the lightly greased rack of an uncovered grill directly over medium heat for 14 to 18 minutes or until juices run clear and no pink remains, turning once.

To serve, spoon the Curry Catsup over the burgers. (Or, lightly grill pita rounds on both sides until toasted, allowing 1 to 2 minutes per side. Cut rounds in half; place burger in each pita half and top with Curry Catsup.)

Curry Catsup: Chop 4 medium plum tomatoes. In medium saucepan combine tomatoes, ½ cup catsup, 3 tablespoons finely chopped onion, 2 tablespoons snipped fresh cilantro, and 2 teaspoons curry powder. Bring to boiling; reduce heat. Simmer, covered, for 5 minutes, stirring occasionally. Season to taste with salt and pepper.

Nutrition facts per serving: 407 cal., 11 g total fat (3 g sat. fat), 95 mg chol., 1,113 mg sodium, 52 g carbo., 2 g fiber, 24 g pro. Daily values: 10% vit. A, 33% vit. C, 8% calcium, 27% iron

duck breast with lime sauce

A casual cookout can be elegant, too. Grilled duck breast served with a fruity sauce and a garnish of fresh red raspberries makes beautiful company fare with no fuss.

Prep: 20 minutes   Grill: 10 minutes   Makes 4 servings

In a small saucepan combine jelly, wine, vinegar, lime peel, lime juice, ginger, ⅛ teaspoon salt, and dash pepper. Bring just to boiling; reduce heat. Simmer, uncovered, about 12 minutes or until sauce is slightly thickened and reduced to ½ cup. Remove from heat; stir in margarine. Reserve all but ¼ cup of the jelly mixture.

Meanwhile, rinse duck breasts; pat dry. Brush oil over both sides of duck breasts. Grill duck on the lightly greased rack of an uncovered grill directly over medium heat for 10 to 12 minutes or until tender and no pink remains, turning once and brushing with the ¼ cup jelly mixture during the last 2 to 3 minutes of grilling. Serve duck with the reserved jelly mixture. Garnish with raspberries, if desired.

Nutrition facts per serving: 222 cal., 8 g total fat (2 g sat. fat), 22 mg chol., 124 mg sodium, 29 g carbo., 0 g fiber, 6 g pro. Daily values: 4% vit. A, 5% vit. C, 1% calcium, 8% iron

fowl play

Despite its rich reputation, duck these days is being bred and raised to be both lean and moist. Duck is known for its distinctive flavor. Generally, older and heavier birds are stronger flavored and less tender. Most commercially raised ducks are fed a regulated diet and sold young to produce sweet and tender meat. Duck is available both fresh and frozen.

43

- ½ cup currant jelly
- ¼ cup sweet or semi-dry white wine, such as Riesling or sauterne
- 1 tablespoon raspberry vinegar
- 1 teaspoon finely shredded lime peel
- 1 tablespoon lime juice
- ¼ teaspoon grated fresh ginger
- 1 tablespoon margarine or butter
- 4 skinless, boneless duck or chicken breast halves (about 1 pound total)
- 2 teaspoons olive oil
  Fresh red raspberries (optional)

Serving suggestion:

Round out this elegant duck dinner with steamed asparagus and whole wheat rolls with herbed butter.

fresh
catches

grilled rosemary trout
with lemon butter

Taste the delicious reason lemon and butter are the timeless, classic accompaniments to fish! This recipe is so simple you'll want to tote it along on your next fishing trip. Spicy Potato Slices (page 70) can be grilled alongside the fish.

Prep: 15 minutes   Grill: 6 minutes   Makes 4 servings

In a small bowl stir together the butter, lemon peel, and half of the shallots; season with salt and coarsely ground black pepper. Set aside.

Rinse fish; pat dry. Spread each fish open. Place fish skin sides down. Rub remaining shallots and the rosemary onto fish; sprinkle with additional salt and pepper and drizzle with lemon juice and oil. Grill fish, skin sides down, on the lightly greased rack of an uncovered grill directly over medium heat for 6 to 8 minutes or until fish flakes easily when tested with a fork.

Meanwhile, place tomatoes, cut sides up, on grill rack; dot each with ¼ teaspoon of the butter mixture. Grill for 5 minutes or until tomatoes are heated through. Remove fish and tomatoes from the grill. Cut each fish in half lengthwise. In a small saucepan melt remaining butter mixture; serve with fish and tomatoes. Sprinkle fish with parsley.

Nutrition facts per serving: 206 cal., 10 g total fat (3 g sat. fat), 75 mg chol., 109 mg sodium, 4 g carbo., 1 g fiber, 24 g pro. Daily values: 13% vit. A, 31% vit. C, 7% calcium, 17% iron

Note: A pan-dressed fish has had the scales and internal organs removed; often the head, fins, and tail also have been removed.

4 **teaspoons butter, softened**

1 **teaspoon finely shredded lemon peel**

1 **tablespoon finely chopped shallots or onion**

2 **fresh rainbow trout, pan dressed and boned (8 to 10 ounces each)***

1 **tablespoon snipped fresh rosemary**

1 **tablespoon lemon juice**

2 **teaspoons olive oil**

2 **medium tomatoes, halved crosswise**

1 **tablespoon snipped fresh parsley**

Serving suggestion:

This classic trout-and-potatoes dinner calls for an equally classic dessert: Try Nectarine-Raspberry Crisp (page 83).

sea bass with black bean & avocado relish

This island-style fish dish draws on the best of Cuba—the land itself (black beans, avocado, and lime) and the water that surrounds it (sea bass). Serve it with a splash of fruit juice, such as pineapple, mango, or papaya, stirred with sparkling water.

4 4- to 5-ounce fresh sea bass fillets, ¾ to 1 inch thick

2 tablespoons snipped fresh cilantro

2 tablespoons snipped fresh oregano

½ teaspoon finely shredded lime peel

2 tablespoons lime juice

1 tablespoon olive oil

¼ to ½ teaspoon bottled hot pepper sauce

1 clove garlic, minced

1 15-ounce can black beans, rinsed and drained

1 avocado, seeded, peeled, and diced

Serving suggestion:

If you want a little something extra on the plate, consider sweet and spicy Honey-Glazed Bananas (page 74).

Prep: 15 minutes   Grill: 4 to 6 minutes per ½-inch thickness

Makes 4 servings

Rinse fish; pat dry. Measure thickness of fish; set aside. In a small bowl stir together cilantro, oregano, lime peel, lime juice, oil, pepper sauce, and garlic. Place 2 tablespoons cilantro mixture in a medium bowl. Add beans and avocado; toss lightly to coat. Cover and refrigerate while cooking fish.

Brush remaining cilantro mixture over fish. Grill fish on the lightly greased rack of an uncovered grill directly over medium heat until fish flakes easily when tested with a fork, turning once. (Allow 4 to 6 minutes per ½-inch thickness of fish.) Serve with bean mixture.

Nutrition facts per serving: 303 cal., 15 g total fat (2 g sat. fat), 47 mg chol., 348 mg sodium, 20 g carbo., 6 g fiber, 29 g pro. Daily values: 9% vit. A, 16% vit. C, 4% calcium, 13% iron

grilled swordfish
with spicy tomato sauce

This vibrant and fresh example of the best of fusion cooking combines two popular Sicilian foods, swordfish and a spicy, fresh tomato sauce, with couscous, a North African favorite.

Prep: 15 minutes   Grill: 8 minutes   Makes 4 servings

Rinse fish; pat dry. Drizzle 2 teaspoons of the oil over swordfish. Sprinkle with ¼ teaspoon each of salt and black pepper. Grill on the lightly greased rack of an uncovered grill directly over medium heat for 8 to 12 minutes or until fish flakes easily when tested with a fork; turn once.

Meanwhile, for the spicy tomato sauce, in a medium skillet heat the remaining oil. Add onion, serrano or jalapeño pepper, garlic, turmeric, and coriander; cook about 2 minutes or until onions are tender. Stir in tomatoes and ¼ teaspoon salt; cook 2 to 3 minutes or until tomatoes are just tender. Remove from heat; stir in cilantro. Serve spicy tomato sauce over fish. If desired, serve with couscous.

Nutrition facts per serving: 237 cal., 11 g total fat (2 g sat. fat), 56 mg chol., 402 mg sodium, 5 g carbo., 1 g fiber, 29 g pro. Daily values: 9% vit. A, 39% vit. C, 1% calcium, 11% iron

fish-grilling **101**
Fillets of fish can break apart easily, so it helps to place them on foil or in a grill basket for grilling. To keep the fish from sticking, lightly brush the foil or basket with cooking oil before adding the fish. To avoid the fish poaching in its own juices during grilling, cut slits in the foil to allow the juices to run through. Firmer-textured fish cut into steaks—such as salmon, halibut, and swordfish—are grilled easily on a lightly greased grill rack.

4 fresh swordfish steaks, 1 inch thick (about 1¼ pounds)

4 teaspoons cooking oil

¼ cup chopped onion

1 small serrano or jalapeño pepper, seeded and finely chopped

½ teaspoon bottled minced garlic

½ teaspoon ground turmeric

¼ teaspoon ground coriander

1½ cups chopped plum tomatoes

1 tablespoon snipped fresh cilantro

Hot cooked couscous (optional)

Serving suggestion:

Start this elegant swordfish dinner with a simple appetizer of Italian black or green olives and pieces of crisp lavosh.

wasabi-glazed whitefish with vegetable slaw

Though its presence in this recipe is subtle, fans of fiery wasabi—the bright-green Japanese horseradish condiment—will notice its head-clearing heat. Wasabi is found in powdered or paste form in Japanese markets or in larger supermarkets.

Prep: 15 minutes   Grill: 6 minutes   Makes 4 servings

Rinse fish; pat dry. In small bowl combine soy sauce, wasabi powder, ½ teaspoon of the sesame oil, and ¼ teaspoon of the sugar. Brush soy mixture over fish. Grill fish on the lightly greased rack of an uncovered grill directly over medium heat for 6 to 9 minutes or until fish flakes easily when tested with a fork, turning after 4 minutes.

Meanwhile, for vegetable slaw, in medium bowl combine the zucchini, radishes, pea pods, and 2 tablespoons of the chives. Stir together the remaining sesame oil, remaining sugar, and vinegar. Drizzle over the zucchini mixture; toss to combine. Sprinkle remaining chives over fish. Serve fish with vegetable slaw.

Nutrition facts per serving: 141 cal., 3 g total fat (1 g sat. fat), 60 mg chol., 363 mg sodium, 6 g carbo., 1 g fiber, 24 g pro. Daily values: 3% vit. A, 46% vit. C, 3% calcium, 10% iron

Note: Use whitefish, sea bass, orange roughy, or any other similar fish fillets.

- 4 4-ounce fresh white-fleshed skinless fish fillets, about ¾ inch thick*
- 2 tablespoons light soy sauce
- ¼ teaspoon wasabi powder or 1 tablespoon prepared horseradish
- 1 teaspoon toasted sesame oil
- ½ teaspoon sugar
- 1 medium zucchini, coarsely shredded (about 1⅓ cups)
- 1 cup sliced radishes
- 1 cup fresh pea pods
- 3 tablespoons snipped fresh chives
- 3 tablespoons rice vinegar

Serving suggestion:

Finish this dinner with Grilled Pineapple with Sugared Wontons (page 89).

grilled tuna with wilted spinach

Tuna bears watching as it cooks because it easily can dry out. Here, a beautiful bed of tiny grape tomatoes and fresh spinach is quick-cooked in a skillet on the grill right next to the tuna—so you can keep your fish under a watchful eye.

1¼ **pounds fresh skinless tuna fillets,**
about ¾ inch thick

3 **tablespoons balsamic vinegar**

1 **tablespoon olive oil**

¼ **teaspoon garlic pepper**

1 **medium red onion,**
sliced ¼ inch thick

2 **cups grape tomatoes or cherry**
tomatoes, halved

6 **cups torn fresh spinach**
or torn mixed greens

2 **tablespoons water**

Serving suggestion:

Toss hot couscous with some toasted pine nuts and fresh herbs for a delicious accompaniment.

**Prep: 15 minutes   Marinate: 5 minutes
Grill: 6 minutes   Makes 4 servings**

Rinse fish; pat dry. Cut fish into 4 portions. Lightly sprinkle with salt and pepper; place in shallow dish. In small mixing bowl stir together the vinegar, oil, garlic pepper, and ¼ teaspoon salt. Pour 2 tablespoons of the vinegar mixture over fish. Cover and marinate at room temperature for 5 minutes. Drain fish, reserving marinade. Grill fish and onion slices on lightly greased rack of an uncovered grill directly over medium heat for 6 to 9 minutes or until fish flakes easily when tested with a fork, turning and brushing with reserved marinade after 4 minutes.

While the fish is cooking, in a large heavy skillet* toss together the tomatoes, spinach, and water. Place skillet on grill rack directly over medium heat. Cook 3 to 4 minutes or until spinach begins to wilt, stirring occasionally. Transfer spinach mixture to serving platter; place fish and onion slices atop. Drizzle with remaining vinegar mixture.

Nutrition facts per serving: 299 cal., 11 g total fat (2 g sat. fat), 59 mg chol., 315 mg sodium, 10 g carbo., 3 g fiber, 39 g pro. Daily values: 134% vit. A, 58% vit. C, 6% calcium, 26% iron

Note: The heat from the grill will blacken the outside of the skillet, so use a cast-iron or old skillet.

minty grilled halibut with yellow squash

When you're truly pressed for time, but still crave something light and healthy, try this delicious fish. Flavored with fresh basil and mint and served with smoky, grilled summer squash, it's ready from start to finish in about 20 minutes!

Prep: 15 minutes   Grill: 8 minutes   Makes 4 servings

Rinse fish; pat dry. In a small bowl whisk together the lemon juice, oil, and garlic. Reserve 3 tablespoons of the mixture. Brush remaining lemon juice mixture on fish and the cut sides of the squash. Lightly sprinkle fish and squash with salt and pepper. Grill fish on the lightly greased rack of an uncovered grill directly over medium heat for 8 to 12 minutes or until fish flakes easily when tested with a fork, turning once. During the last 5 to 6 minutes of grilling, grill the squash until just tender, turning once.

Meanwhile, stir basil and mint into the reserved lemon juice mixture.

Transfer the squash to a cutting board; cool slightly and slice ⅛ inch to ¼ inch thick. Place squash on a serving platter; drizzle with some of the basil mixture. Top with fish; drizzle with the remaining basil mixture.

Nutrition facts per serving: 233 cal., 10 g total fat (1 g sat. fat), 46 mg chol., 112 mg sodium, 5 g carbo., 1 g fiber, 30 g pro. Daily values: 8% vit. A, 19% vit. C, 7% calcium, 11% iron

1¼ to 1½ pounds fresh halibut or
    salmon steaks, 1 inch thick

¼ cup lemon juice

2 tablespoons olive oil

3 cloves garlic, minced

2 medium yellow summer squash
   or zucchini, halved lengthwise

2 tablespoons finely snipped
   fresh basil

1 tablespoon snipped fresh mint

Serving suggestion:

Serve this speedy entrée with chewy Italian bread and follow it up with strawberries tossed with lemon juice and sugar and sprinkled with freshly ground black pepper.

dilly salmon fillets

A quick, dill-infused, Dijon-flavored mayonnaise caps off these Scandinavian-style salmon fillets. For a built-in salad and extra freshness, serve them on a bed of shredded cucumber.

4 6-ounce fresh skinless salmon
    fillets, ½ to ¾ inch thick

3 tablespoons lemon juice

2 tablespoons snipped fresh dill

2 tablespoons mayonnaise
    or salad dressing

2 teaspoons Dijon-style mustard

   Dash freshly ground black pepper

Serving suggestion:

*Fill out this flavorful salmon
dinner with Jasmine-Mint
Tea Rice with Peas (page 71).*

Prep: 15 minutes   Marinate: 10 minutes
Grill: 5 minutes   Makes 4 servings

Rinse fish; pat dry and place in a shallow dish. In a small bowl combine the lemon juice and 1 tablespoon of the dill; pour over fish and marinate at room temperature for 10 minutes. Meanwhile, in a small bowl stir together the remaining dill, the mayonnaise, mustard, and pepper; set aside.

In a grill with a cover arrange preheated coals around drip pan. Test for medium heat above pan. Place the fish on the lightly greased grill rack over the drip pan. Cover and grill for 3 minutes. Turn fish; spread the mayonnaise mixture atop the fish. Cover and grill 2 to 6 minutes more or until fish flakes easily when tested with a fork.

Nutrition facts per serving: 211 cal., 11 g total fat (2 g sat. fat), 35 mg chol., 204 mg sodium, 1 g carbo., 0 g fiber, 25 g pro. Daily values: 4% vit. A, 8% vit. C, 1% calcium, 7% iron

red snapper with fresh herb-pecan crust

Butter, chopped pecans, fresh herbs, and a touch of lemon and garlic make a toasty crust on this meaty grilled red snapper. Instead of Italian parsley, you can substitute your favorite herb. It's terrific on fresh walleye, too!

2 tablespoons margarine or butter, softened

⅓ cup finely chopped pecans

2 tablespoons fine dry bread crumbs

1 teaspoon finely shredded lemon peel

2 garlic cloves, minced

1 tablespoon snipped fresh Italian parsley

¼ teaspoon salt

⅛ teaspoon black pepper

Dash ground red pepper

4 5- or 6-ounce red snapper fillets with skin

Lemon wedges (optional)

Serving suggestion:

A bed of grilled zucchini and summer squash slices makes a pretty presentation for these fillets—or try a side of Grilled Corn Relish (page 81) and sourdough bread.

Prep: 15 minutes   Grill: 4 to 6 minutes per ½-inch thickness
Makes 4 servings

Rinse fish; pat dry. Measure thickness of fish; set aside. In a small bowl combine margarine, pecans, bread crumbs, lemon peel, garlic, the 1 tablespoon parsley, salt, black pepper, and red pepper. Place fish, skin side down, on the greased rack of an uncovered grill directly over medium coals. Spoon pecan mixture on top of fillets; spread slightly. Grill fish 4 to 6 minutes per ½-inch thickness, or until fish flakes easily with a fork. Transfer to a serving platter with a wide spatula. Sprinkle fish with additional snipped parsley and serve with lemon wedges, if desired.

Nutrition facts per serving: 268 cal., 14 g total fat (2 g sat. fat), 52 mg chol., 287 mg sodium, 7 g carbo., .8 g fiber, 30 g pro. Daily values: 7% vit. A, 4% vit. C, 4% calcium, 4% iron

direct versus indirect

Direct grilling means food is placed on the rack directly over the coals. This method is often used for fast-cooking foods such as burgers, steaks, boneless chicken, fish, and seafood. Indirect grilling means a covered grill acts as an oven. A disposable drip pan is placed in the center of the charcoal grate and hot coals are arranged around it. This method is used for slower-cooking foods, such as roasts or bone-in poultry. Because of their speed, most of the recipes in this book call for direct grilling. See the grilling charts on pages 90 to 93 for timings.

scallop brochettes

A little bit sweet, a little bit tangy, these seafood brochettes, soaked in a simple marinade of sherry, mustard, honey, and soy sauce, can be made with scallops, shrimp, or a combination of both.

Prep: 15 minutes   Marinate: 30 minutes
Grill: 6 minutes   Makes 4 servings

Halve large scallops (you should have about 20 pieces). Place scallops in a plastic bag set in a shallow dish. For marinade, in a small bowl combine oil, sherry, mustard, honey, and soy sauce. Pour over the scallops. Close bag; marinate in the refrigerator for 30 minutes.

Drain the scallops, discarding the marinade. Thread scallops on long metal skewers. (If using scallops and shrimp, thread a scallop in the "curl" of each shrimp.) Grill on the lightly greased rack of an uncovered grill directly over medium heat for 6 to 8 minutes or until scallops are opaque; turn once.

Nutrition facts per serving: 119 cal., 5 g total fat (1 g saturated fat), 34 mg chol., 284 mg sodium, 4 g carb., 0 g fiber, 15 g pro. Daily values: 0% vit. A, 0% vit. C, 6% calcium, 13% iron

1 **pound sea scallops and/or**
  peeled and deveined shrimp

2 **tablespoons cooking oil**

2 **tablespoons dry sherry**

2 **tablespoons stone-ground mustard**

1 **tablespoon honey**

1½ **teaspoons soy sauce**

Serving suggestion:

Serve these seafood brochettes on a bed of cold rice vermicelli that has been tossed with a little toasted sesame oil, rice vinegar, and shredded carrots.

rosemary-orange
shrimp kabobs

Bacon-wrapped shrimp sounds decadent, but it can be everyday fare when you use light turkey bacon. Here, the bacon gives the shrimp a subtle smokiness, and a brushed-on herbed orange juice adds a pleasing sweetness.

Prep: 20 minutes Grill: 8 minutes Makes 4 servings

Peel and devein shrimp, leaving tails intact. Rinse shrimp; pat dry. Wrap each shrimp in a half slice of bacon. Alternately thread shrimp and sweet pepper pieces on long metal skewers. In small bowl combine 1 teaspoon of the orange peel, the orange juice, and rosemary. Brush over kabobs.

Grill kabobs on the lightly greased rack of an uncovered grill directly over medium heat for 8 to 10 minutes or until bacon is crisp and shrimp turn pink, turning once.

Meanwhile, in a medium saucepan stir together the remaining peel, cooked rice, and beans; heat through. Serve with shrimp and peppers.

Nutrition facts per serving: 310 cal., 7 g total fat (2 g sat. fat), 149 mg chol., 563 mg sodium, 36 g carbo., 2 g fiber, 26 g pro. Daily values: 20% vit. A, 139% vit. C, 5% calcium, 29% iron

a different kind of **orange**
Blood oranges, also called sanguines or Moro oranges, are becoming increasingly available—and that's a good thing. Sweeter and juicier than most oranges, they get their name from their mottled, deep-red flesh and blushing-red skin. They're wonderful for eating out of hand, and when used in a marinade, impart a rosy hue to foods.

1 **pound large fresh shrimp in shells (about 16 shrimp)**

8 **slices turkey bacon, halved crosswise**

2 **red and/or yellow sweet peppers, cut into 1-inch pieces**

2 **teaspoons finely shredded orange or blood orange peel**

2 **tablespoons orange or blood orange juice**

2 **teaspoons snipped fresh rosemary**

2 **cups hot cooked rice**

1 **cup cooked or canned black beans, rinsed and drained**

Serving suggestion:

Follow these orange-herb-infused shrimp kabobs with coffee-flavored ice cream and chocolate-sauce sundaes.

garden variety grilling

southwestern black bean cakes with guacamole

These spicy bean cakes are finger foods that are filling enough to make a meal. They're flavored with a chipotle—a dried, smoked jalapeño pepper—that comes in adobo sauce, a Mexican melange of ground chili peppers, herbs, and vinegar.

Prep: 20 minutes   Grill: 8 minutes   Makes 4 servings

Place torn bread in a food processor bowl or blender container. Cover and process or blend until bread resembles coarse crumbs; transfer to a large bowl and set aside. Place cilantro and garlic in the food processor bowl or blender container; cover and process or blend until finely chopped. Add beans, 1 of the chipotle peppers, 1 to 2 teaspoons of the adobo sauce (reserve remaining peppers and sauce for another use), and cumin; process or blend using on/off pulses until beans are coarsely chopped and mixture begins to pull away from sides. Add mixture to bread crumbs in bowl. Add egg; mix well and shape into four ½-inch-thick patties.

Grill patties on the lightly greased rack of an uncovered grill directly over medium heat for 8 to 10 minutes or until patties are heated through, turning once.

Meanwhile, for guacamole, in small bowl mash avocado. Stir in lime juice; season with salt and pepper. Serve patties with guacamole and tomato.

Nutrition facts per serving: 178 cal., 7 g total fat (1 g sat. fat), 53 mg chol., 487 mg sodium, 25 g carbo., 9 g fiber, 11 g pro. Daily values: 9% vit. A, 12% vit. C, 7% calcium, 16% iron

- **2 slices whole wheat bread, torn**
- **3 tablespoons fresh cilantro**
- **2 cloves garlic**
- **1 15-ounce can black beans, rinsed and drained**
- **1 7-ounce can chipotle peppers in adobo sauce**
- **1 teaspoon ground cumin**
- **1 egg**
- **½ of a medium avocado, seeded and peeled**
- **1 tablespoon lime juice**
- **1 small plum tomato, chopped**

Serving suggestion:

For burger baskets, place the bean cakes on a bed of purchased baked tortilla chips in a lined basket or bowl and garnish with orange wedges.

tomato ravioli with grilled portobellos & spinach

Rosy-hued purchased sun-dried tomato ravioli are dotted with a fresh green duo of spinach and sweet basil. Slices of smoky, garlic-infused grilled portobello mushrooms are substantial enough you won't notice the absence of meat.

60

2 tablespoons olive oil

2 garlic cloves, minced

4 to 5 large portobello mushrooms (about 1 pound total), stems removed

1 9-ounce package refrigerated cheese-filled sun-dried-tomato-flavored ravioli

4 cups torn fresh spinach

1 tablespoon snipped fresh basil

¼ cup grated Parmesan cheese

¼ teaspoon freshly ground black pepper

Grated Parmesan cheese (optional)

Serving suggestion:

Warm up wedges of focaccia on the grill to nibble alongside this pretty pasta dish.

Prep: 15 minutes   Grill: 10 minutes   Makes 4 servings

Combine 1 tablespoon of the oil and the garlic. Lightly brush rounded side of mushrooms with garlic-oil mixture; sprinkle lightly with salt and pepper. Grill mushrooms on the rack of an uncovered grill directly over medium coals for 10 to 12 minutes or until slightly softened, turning once. Slice the mushrooms into bite-size pieces.

Meanwhile, cook the ravioli in boiling, lightly salted water according to package directions. For the last 1 minute of cooking, add spinach to boiling pasta water; drain. Place ravioli and spinach in a large bowl; add mushrooms. Toss with remaining oil, basil, the ¼ cup Parmesan cheese, and the ¼ teaspoon freshly ground black pepper. If desired, serve with additional grated Parmesan cheese.

Nutrition facts per serving: 336 cal., 18 g total fat (7 g sat. fat), 61 mg chol., 500 mg sodium, 31 g carbo., 3 g fiber, 16 g pro. Daily values: 40% vit. A, 35% vit. C, 25% calcium, 31% iron

bella **portobello!**

Meaty portobello mushrooms are the mature form of the crimino mushroom, a brown variation of the white button mushroom. Portobellos are great for the grill—simply brush them with olive oil and garlic. The grilled result can be eaten like a steak, sliced and tossed with pasta, rolled in a tortilla with grilled red peppers, or slipped between slices of grilled focaccia or bread.

tandoori sweet potatoes with raita & pilau

Sweet potatoes aren't just for Thanksgiving anymore. They're great on the grill in this vegetarian entrée that's spiced with curry butter and served with a cooling yogurt sauce and fruit-and-nut-studded pilau.

Prep: 25 minutes   Grill: 15 minutes   Makes 4 servings

Peel sweet potatoes and cut into ½-inch-thick slices. In a small bowl stir together the melted butter and curry powder. Brush butter mixture onto both sides of the sweet potato slices, reserving any remaining butter mixture. Place the sweet potatoes on the rack of a grill with a cover directly over medium heat; cover and grill for 15 to 18 minutes or until tender, turning occasionally.

Meanwhile, for the pilau, in a large saucepan heat remaining butter mixture over medium heat. Add onion; cook about 3 minutes or until tender. Add the rice; cook and stir for 3 to 4 minutes more or until the rice begins to brown. Carefully add the water. Heat to boiling; reduce heat. Simmer, covered, about 15 minutes or until the liquid is absorbed and the rice is tender. Remove from heat. Stir in apricots, almonds, and salt and pepper to taste. Cover and let stand for 5 minutes.

For the raita, in a small bowl combine the yogurt and cilantro; season with salt and pepper.

Serve the sweet potatoes with the pilau and raita.

Nutrition facts per serving: 499 cal., 14 g total fat (6 g sat. fat), 27 mg chol., 216 mg sodium, 83 g carbo., 8 g fiber, 11 g pro. Daily values: 306% vit. A, 56% vit. C, 16% calcium, 26% iron

2 large or 4 small sweet potatoes or yams (about 1½ pounds total)

3 tablespoons butter, melted

1 to 2 tablespoons curry powder or garam masala (page 27)

1 small onion, chopped

1 cup basmati rice

2 cups water

⅓ cup snipped dried apricots or assorted dried fruit

¼ cup slivered almonds, toasted

1 8-ounce carton plain yogurt

1 tablespoon snipped fresh cilantro

Serving suggestion:

If it's spicy curry powder you crave, cool the fire after dinner with a few scoops of mango sorbet.

saffron pilaf with grilled vegetables

Similar to paella—Spain's national dish—this sunny-colored saffron rice dish is bursting with flavor, but from a rainbow of grilled vegetables instead of the standard shrimp and meat. Serve it with a hearty red wine.

63

Prep: 20 minutes   Grill: 10 minutes   Makes 4 servings

In a large saucepan combine rice, vegetable broth, water, and saffron. Heat to boiling; reduce heat. Simmer, covered, about 15 minutes or until rice is tender and liquid is absorbed; keep warm.

Meanwhile, in a small bowl combine oil and garlic; brush over sweet pepper, zucchini, and eggplant. Grill vegetables on the lightly greased rack of an uncovered grill directly over medium heat about 10 minutes or until tender, turning once. Season with salt and pepper to taste.

Transfer vegetables to cutting board; cool slightly. Cut vegetables into bite-size pieces; stir into cooked rice. Top with goat cheese and nuts.

Nutrition facts per serving: 333 cal., 12 g total fat (2 g sat. fat), 7 mg chol., 443 mg sodium, 48 g carbo., 5 g fiber, 9 g pro. Daily values: 5% vit. A, 40% vit. C, 4% calcium, 20% iron

Note: You may substitute ¼ teaspoon turmeric for the saffron.

- 1 **cup jasmine, basmati, or wild-pecan long grain rice**
- 1 **14½-ounce can vegetable broth**
- ¼ **cup water**
- ⅛ **teaspoon saffron threads or dash ground saffron***
- 2 **tablespoons olive oil**
- ½ **teaspoon bottled minced garlic**
- 1 **red sweet pepper, seeded and quartered**
- 1 **large zucchini, halved lengthwise**
- 1 **eggplant, sliced ½ inch thick**
- 1 **ounce herbed semi-soft goat cheese (chévre), crumbled**
- 2 **tablespoons coarsely chopped hazelnuts or pecans, toasted**

Serving suggestion:

Start an outdoor feast featuring this Spanish-style pilaf with tapas-style appetizers including olives, grilled vegetables, and cubes of piquant cheese.

grilled gazpacho medley open-faced sandwich

Stay as cool as a cucumber with this hearty sandwich featuring the flavors of the cold soup, gazpacho. Tomatoes, garlic, cucumbers, and jalapeños get mixed with black beans, then scooped into grilled French bread "bowls" and topped with cheese.

64

- 1 **medium cucumber, seeded and chopped**
- 1 **cup cooked or canned black beans, rinsed and drained**
- ¼ **cup snipped fresh cilantro**
- 1 **tablespoon olive oil**
- 2 **tablespoons cider vinegar**
- 1 **clove garlic, minced**
- 1 **pickled jalapeño pepper, finely chopped**
- ½ **to 1 teaspoon chili powder**
- 3 **large tomatoes, halved**
- 1 **large sweet onion (such as Vidalia), sliced ½ inch thick**
- 1 **loaf French bread**
- 1 **cup shredded cheddar cheese**

Serving suggestion:

One Mexican-inspired dish deserves another: Satisfy sweet tooths with Grilled Chocolate-Raspberry Burritos (page 85).

Prep: 20 minutes   Grill: 13 minutes   Makes 6 servings

In a medium bowl combine the cucumber, beans, cilantro, oil, vinegar, garlic, jalapeño, chili powder, and salt and pepper to taste. Set aside.

Place the tomatoes and onion slices on the lightly greased rack of a grill with a cover directly over medium heat; grill, uncovered, for 12 to 15 minutes or until lightly charred, turning onion slices once. Transfer vegetables to a cutting board; cool slightly and coarsely chop. Add chopped vegetables to the cucumber mixture; toss to combine.

Meanwhile, halve the French bread lengthwise. Cut each bread half crosswise into 3 pieces. Using a fork, hollow out the bread pieces slightly. Grill the bread pieces, cut sides down, about 1 minute or until toasted. Spoon the bean mixture into the bread pieces; sprinkle sandwiches with cheddar cheese. Place the sandwiches on the grill rack, filled sides up; close lid and grill for 1 to 2 minutes or until cheese is melted.

Nutrition facts per serving: 329 cal., 11 g total fat (5 g sat. fat), 20 mg chol., 634 mg sodium, 46 g carbo., 3 g fiber, 14 g pro. Daily values: 12% vit. A, 19% vit. C, 17% calcium, 18% iron

spaghetti squash with grilled plum tomatoes

If you've never tried spaghetti squash, here's a delightful way to get acquainted. The cooked flesh of this creamy-yellow squash separates into toothsome, spaghetti-like strands. What better way to eat it than topped with a grilled-tomato sauce?

Prep: 15 minutes   Microwave: 10 minutes
Grill: 10 minutes   Makes 4 to 6 servings

Place squash, cut sides down, in a microwave-safe 2-quart rectangular baking dish; add the water. Prick skin all over with a fork. Cover with vented plastic wrap. Microwave on 100% power (high) about 10 minutes or until squash is tender. Let squash stand for 5 minutes.

Combine oil, Italian seasoning, salt, and pepper. Using fork, remove pulp from squash shells, separating it into strands. Transfer to bowl; toss with 2 teaspoons of the oil mixture and the Parmesan cheese. Fold a 36×18-inch piece of heavy foil in half to make a double thickness of foil that measures 18×18 inches. Place squash mixture in center of foil. Bring up opposite edges of foil and seal with double fold. Fold remaining edges to completely enclose the squash mixture, leaving space for steam to build. Grill squash packet on the rack of an uncovered grill directly over medium heat for 10 minutes, turning once. Toss tomatoes with remaining oil mixture. For last 5 minutes of grilling, place tomatoes on grill rack beside packet. Grill tomatoes just until tender, turning once. Transfer tomatoes to cutting board; cool slightly and chop. Spoon over squash; sprinkle with basil.

Nutrition facts per serving: 133 cal., 8 g total fat (1 g sat. fat), 10 mg chol., 447 mg sodium, 9 g carbo., 2 g fiber, 6 g pro. Daily values: 6% vit. A, 25% vit. C, 12% calcium, 5% iron

1 2½-pound spaghetti squash, halved lengthwise and seeded

2 tablespoons water

4 teaspoons olive oil

1 teaspoon dried Italian seasoning

½ teaspoon salt

¼ teaspoon pepper

½ cup finely shredded Parmesan cheese

4 medium red and/or yellow plum tomatoes, quartered

2 tablespoons snipped fresh basil

Serving suggestion:

Round out this healthy vegetarian meal with Piquant Grilled Broccoli & Olives (page 77) and grilled whole wheat Italian country bread.

grilled sicilian-style pizza

Sicilians like their escarole—a mild, leafy kind of endive—sautéed with lots of olive oil and served with chewy bread to sop up the juices. For maximum flavor in this grilled adaptation of that idea, use the tangy Italian cheese, Pecorino Romano.

1 **16-ounce Italian bread shell (Boboli)**

2 **plum tomatoes, thinly sliced**

1 **large yellow or red tomato, thinly sliced**

4 **ounces fresh mozzarella or buffalo mozzarella cheese, thinly sliced**

⅓ **cup halved, pitted kalamata olives**

1 **tablespoon olive oil**

1 **cup coarsely chopped escarole or curly endive**

¼ **cup shredded Pecorino Romano or Parmesan cheese (1 ounce)**

Serving suggestion:

Finish this meal-in-one with a flourish. Serve with purchased biscotti and a little sweet wine— such as Vin Santo—or espresso or cappuccino for dipping.

Prep: 20 minutes   Grill: 8 minutes   Makes 4 servings

Top bread shell with tomatoes, mozzarella cheese, and olives. Drizzle oil over all. Fold a 24×18-inch piece of heavy foil in half lengthwise. Place on foil, turning edges of foil up to edge of pizza.

In a grill with a cover arrange preheated coals around a drip pan for indirect grilling. Test for medium heat above pan. Place pizza on the grill rack over the drip pan. Cover and grill about 8 minutes or until pizza is heated through, topping with escarole the last 2 minutes of grilling. To serve, sprinkle cheese and freshly ground black pepper over pizza.

Nutrition facts per serving: 459 cal., 19 g total fat (4 g sat. fat), 26 mg chol., 893 mg sodium, 54 g carbo., 3 g fiber, 24 g pro. Daily values:12% vit. A, 14% vit. C, 31% calcium, 18% iron

fresh is best

They may have the same last name, but the similarity ends there. Fresh mozzarella—made from whole milk—has a much softer texture and sweeter, more delicate flavor than regular mozzarella, which is made in low-fat and nonfat versions and is aged to give it a longer shelf life. Fresh mozzarella, usually packaged in whey or water and shaped into irregular balls, must be eaten within a few days of purchase. It's available in Italian markets and cheese shops and increasingly, in many supermarkets.

simple
sides

grilled antipasto skewers

Not really onions at all—but sometimes called wild onions—cipollini are actually the bittersweet bulbs of the grape hyacinth. Fresh cipollini are available mostly in late summer and fall. If you can't find them at your supermarket, check at Italian markets.

Prep: 25 minutes Grill: 8 minutes Makes 6 servings

In a small saucepan bring vinegar to boiling; reduce heat. Simmer, uncovered, for 5 minutes or until vinegar is reduced to 3 tablespoons. Set aside to cool.

Drain artichoke hearts, reserving 2 tablespoons liquid; set aside. On 4 long metal skewers alternately thread peppers, cipollini, and mushrooms, leaving ¼ inch between pieces. In a small bowl combine reduced vinegar and reserved artichoke liquid. Brush half of vinegar mixture over vegetables.

Grill skewers on the rack of an uncovered grill directly over medium heat for 8 to 10 minutes or until vegetables are tender, turning once and brushing often with remaining vinegar mixture. Remove vegetables from skewers and transfer to a large bowl; add drained artichokes, cheese, and basil. Season with salt and pepper to taste. Toss gently to combine.

Nutrition facts per serving: 106 cal., 4 g total fat (2 g sat. fat), 7 mg chol., 220 mg sodium, 14 g carbo., 1 g fiber, 4 g pro. Daily values: 18% vit. A, 94% vit. C, 7% calcium, 9% iron

⅓ cup balsamic vinegar

1 6½-ounce jar marinated artichoke hearts

1 medium red sweet pepper, cut into 1-inch pieces

1 medium yellow sweet pepper, cut into 1-inch pieces

8 small whole or 4 medium cipollini, halved, or 8 pearl onions

8 large crimini or button mushrooms, stems removed

2 ounces provolone cheese, cut into thin short strips

¼ cup snipped fresh basil

spicy potato slices

Potatoes with a buttery yellow flesh, such as Yukon gold or Finnish yellow, are ideal for this dish. The spices are a nice contrast to their moist, creamy texture. Gild the lily with a little light sour cream and snipped chives, if you like.

1 teaspoon dried thyme, crushed

½ teaspoon paprika

½ teaspoon garlic salt

⅛ teaspoon freshly ground black pepper

3 large yellow potatoes or 2 russet potatoes, scrubbed (about 1 pound)

1 sweet onion (such as Vidalia or Walla Walla), sliced

2 tablespoons olive oil

¼ cup light dairy sour cream (optional)

1 tablespoon snipped fresh chives (optional)

Prep: 10 minutes   Grill: 20 minutes   Makes 4 servings

For seasoning mixture, combine thyme, paprika, garlic salt, and pepper; set aside. Fold a 36×18-inch piece of heavy foil in half to make a double thickness of foil that measures 18×18 inches. Cut potatoes crosswise into ¼-inch-thick slices. Place the potato slices and onion slices in the center of the foil. Drizzle with oil. Sprinkle with seasoning mixture.

Bring up opposite edges of foil and seal with a double fold. Fold remaining edges to completely enclose the vegetables, leaving space for steam to build.

Grill on the rack of an uncovered grill directly over medium heat for 20 to 25 minutes or until potatoes are tender. If desired, serve with the sour cream and chives.

Nutrition facts per serving: 186 cal., 7 g total fat (1 g sat. fat), 0 mg chol., 266 mg sodium, 29 g carbo., 1 g fiber, 3 g pro. Daily values: 1% vit. A, 29% vit. C, 1% calcium, 11% iron

jasmine-mint tea rice with peas

Here's an interesting idea: You might know that cooking rice in stock or broth gives it extra flavor, but how about in tea? Here, nutty, aromatic jasmine rice is cooked in mint tea—and tossed with fresh mint and peas. Serve it with grilled fish or lamb.

Start to finish: 32 minutes   Makes 4 servings

Place tea bag in a small glass bowl. Pour boiling water over tea. Cover; let stand 5 minutes. Remove tea bag and discard. Meanwhile, tear off a 36×18-inch piece of heavy foil. Fold in half to make a double thickness of foil that measures 18×18 inches. Bring up all sides of foil to form a pouch. Place uncooked rice in center of pouch. Place margarine or butter on top of rice; sprinkle with salt. Carefully pour brewed tea over rice. Bring edges of foil together and seal tightly, forming a pouch, leaving space for steam to build. Grill foil pouch on the rack of an uncovered grill directly over medium-high coals about 25 minutes or until liquid is absorbed and rice is tender. Remove from grill. Carefully open packet. Add peas. Seal packet and let stand 10 minutes. Just before serving, sprinkle with fresh mint.

Nutrition facts per serving: 184 cal., 0 g total fat, 0 mg chol., 270 mg sodium,
40 g carbo., 1 g fiber, 4 g pro. Daily values: 1% vit. A, 4% vit. C, 1% calcium, 16% iron

1	bag mint-flavored tea
1¼	cups boiling water
1	cup jasmine rice
1	tablespoon margarine or butter
½	teaspoon salt
½	cup fresh shelled or thawed frozen peas
2	teaspoons snipped fresh mint

nicer rice

Aromatic rices are a bit more expensive than plain white rice, but their qualities are well worth the price. Here's a sampling:

basmati: The nutlike flavor of this very fragrant rice comes from the fact that it's aged to decrease its moisture content.

jasmine: A Thai rice that's similar to basmati but less expensive.

texmati: A cross between American long grain rice and basmati.

wild pecan: An aromatic rice grown in Louisiana with a rich, nutty flavor and a fragrance that resembles freshly popped popcorn.

warm asparagus, fennel, & spinach salad

This beautiful and sophisticated green-on-green salad may be monochromatic to the eye, but its components distinguish themselves on the palate: mild, licoricelike fennel; a variety of mixed greens; and tender, smoky-sweet asparagus.

Prep: 10 minutes   Microwave: 4 minutes
Grill: 12 minutes   Makes 4 servings

Trim off stem end of fennel; quarter fennel but do not remove core. Place fennel in a small microwave-safe dish or pie plate. Add the water. Cover with vented plastic wrap. Microwave on 100% power (high) about 4 minutes or until nearly tender; drain.

Meanwhile, for dressing, in small bowl combine oil, lemon peel, lemon juice, ¼ teaspoon salt, and ⅛ teaspoon pepper; whisk until smooth. Brush fennel and asparagus with 1 tablespoon of the dressing; set remaining dressing aside.

Grill fennel on the rack of an uncovered grill directly over medium heat for 5 minutes, turning occasionally. Add asparagus to the grill; grill vegetables for 7 to 8 minutes more or until vegetables are tender, turning occasionally.

Transfer fennel to a cutting board; cool slightly and slice into ¼- to ½-inch-thick slices, discarding core. Divide fennel and asparagus among 4 dinner plates. Arrange spinach on top. Drizzle with remaining dressing. Top with Parmesan cheese and basil.

Nutrition facts per serving: 111 cal., 9 g total fat (1 g sat. fat), 5 mg chol., 231 mg sodium, 5 g carbo., 7 g fiber, 4 g pro. Daily values: 4% vit. A, 23% vit. C, 7% calcium, 3% iron

1 **medium fennel bulb (about 1 pound)**

2 **tablespoons water**

2 **tablespoons olive oil**

¼ **teaspoon finely shredded lemon peel**

4 **teaspoons lemon juice**

8 **ounces asparagus spears, trimmed**

4 **cups fresh spinach**

¼ **cup shredded Parmesan cheese (1 ounce)**

1 **tablespoon thinly sliced fresh basil**

honey-glazed bananas

Take bananas beyond the lunch box! A little bit sweet and buttery, a little bit tongue-tingling, these grilled bananas are terrific with grilled island-style fish, such as Sea Bass with Black Bean & Avocado Relish (page 46).

2 tablespoons margarine
or butter, melted

1 tablespoon honey

1 teaspoon white vinegar

⅛ teaspoon ground red pepper

2 large ripe, yet firm, bananas
or plantains

Prep: 5 minutes   Grill: 4 minutes   Makes 4 servings

In a small bowl combine margarine, honey, vinegar, and red pepper. Peel bananas or plantains; cut in half lengthwise. Brush generously with honey mixture. Grill on the rack of an uncovered grill directly over medium heat about 4 minutes for bananas (8 minutes for plantains) or until browned and warmed through; turn once and brush often with remaining honey mixture.

Nutrition facts per serving: 133 cal., 6 g total fat (1 g sat. fat), 0 mg chol., 68 mg sodium, 21 g carbo., 1 g fiber, 1 g pro. Daily values: 7% vit. A, 10% vit. C, 0% calcium, 1% iron

yes, we cook with **bananas!**
Bananas or plantains (a large, firm Latin American variety) can be cooked in various stages of ripeness, but are best for the grill when they are ripe yet still firm. For bananas, this means when they are an overall yellow color with a few brown speckles and slightly green tips. Plantains take about a week at room temperature to turn from totally green to yellow-brown and another week or two until they're black and fully ripe. They grill best when they're somewhere between almost black and black.

sweet & spicy pepper-pineapple salsa

To make this colorful salsa quickly, buy the peeled fresh pineapple that's available now in most grocery stores. The zippy condiment perks up grilled beef (try it with Jerk London Broil, page 9) and pork particularly well.

Prep: 15 minutes   Grill: 13 minutes   Makes 6 servings

Grill the pineapple, sweet peppers, and onion on the rack of an uncovered grill directly over medium heat for 10 to 12 minutes or until sweet peppers are slightly charred, turning once. Transfer pineapple and vegetables to a cutting board; cool slightly and coarsely chop.

Meanwhile, in a medium saucepan* combine jam, vinegar, salt, cinnamon, allspice, and hot pepper sauce. Place saucepan over heat near edge of grill. Cook and stir for 3 to 5 minutes or until jam is melted. Add the chopped pineapple, sweet peppers, and onion to the pan. Serve warm or at room temperature over grilled meats or poultry.

Nutrition facts per serving: 76 cal., 0 g total fat (0 g sat. fat), 0 mg chol., 93 mg sodium, 20 g carbo., 1 g fiber, 1 g pro. Daily values: 13% vit. A, 81% vit. C, 1% calcium, 3% iron

Note: The heat from the grill will blacken the outside of the saucepan, so use an old one or a small cast-iron skillet.

12 ounces peeled and cored fresh pineapple, sliced ½ inch thick

2 large red and/or green sweet peppers, seeded and quartered

1 ½-inch-thick slice sweet onion (such as Vidalia or Walla Walla)

¼ cup apricot jam

2 tablespoons rice vinegar

¼ teaspoon salt

¼ teaspoon ground cinnamon

¼ teaspoon ground allspice

¼ teaspoon bottled hot pepper sauce

piquant grilled
broccoli & olives

Broccoli on the grill? You bet! The grilled flowerets take on a pleasing smokiness and still stay crisp-tender. This intensely flavored side dish goes great with any grilled meat or poultry—or toss it with hot cooked pasta for a vegetarian entrée.

77

Prep: 15 minutes   Marinate: 10 minutes
Grill: 6 minutes   Makes 4 servings

In a large saucepan bring a small amount of water to boiling; add broccoli. Simmer, covered, for 2 minutes. Drain well. In a medium bowl combine broccoli and olives. For marinade, in a small bowl whisk together anchovies (if using), oregano, vinegar, oil, garlic, red pepper, and salt. Pour the marinade over the broccoli and olives. Marinate at room temperature for 10 minutes, stirring occasionally. Drain broccoli; discard marinade.

On long metal skewers alternately thread broccoli flowerets and olives. Grill on the rack of an uncovered grill directly over medium heat for 6 to 8 minutes or until broccoli is lightly browned and tender, turning occasionally.

Nutrition facts per serving: 91 cal., 8 g total fat (1 g sat. fat), 0 mg chol., 125 mg sodium, 6 g carbo., 3 g fiber, 3 g pro. Daily values: 13% vit. A, 121% vit. C, 4% calcium, 6% iron

3½ **cups broccoli flowerets**

½ **cup pitted ripe olives**

½ **of a 2-ounce can anchovy fillets, drained and finely chopped (optional)**

2 **tablespoons snipped fresh oregano or Italian flat parsley**

2 **tablespoons red wine vinegar**

2 **tablespoons olive oil**

5 **cloves garlic, minced**

½ **teaspoon crushed red pepper**

Dash salt

couscous with grilled vegetables

Serve this pretty lemon-scented vegetable couscous with something uncomplicated, such as grilled chicken or pork, to show off its lovely hues and fresh flavors.

¼ cup snipped fresh oregano

¼ cup snipped fresh parsley

¼ cup lemon juice

3 tablespoons olive oil

1 teaspoon bottled minced garlic

1 tablespoon water

2 red and/or green sweet peppers,
   seeded and quartered

1 medium red onion, sliced
   ½ inch thick

1 small zucchini, halved lengthwise

1 small yellow summer squash,
   halved lengthwise

1 10-ounce package couscous

½ cup pistachio nuts or dry roasted
   peanuts (optional)

Prep: 20 minutes   Grill: 12 minutes   Makes 6 to 8 servings

For dressing, in a small bowl combine oregano, parsley, lemon juice, oil, garlic, and water. Brush the vegetables lightly with some of the dressing. Grill the vegetables on the rack of an uncovered grill directly over medium heat for 12 to 15 minutes or until vegetables are crisp-tender, turning occasionally.

Meanwhile, prepare the couscous according to package directions. Transfer grilled vegetables to cutting board; cool slightly and coarsely chop. Add chopped vegetables to couscous. Stir in remaining dressing. If desired, stir in nuts. Season to taste with salt and freshly ground black pepper; toss.

Nutrition facts per serving: 259 cal., 7 g total fat (1 g sat. fat), 0 mg chol., 32 mg sodium, 42 g carbo., 8 g fiber, 7 g pro. Daily values: 12% vit. A, 67% vit. C, 2% calcium, 6% iron

grilled eggplant salad

Few vegetables take to the grill so kindly as eggplant. Its meaty flesh stays firm with grilling, and it tastes delicious with the smoky flavor grilling imparts. You can use the smaller, rounder Italian or baby eggplant in place of the Japanese variety.

Prep: 10 minutes   Grill: 8 minutes   Makes 4 to 6 servings

In a small bowl combine the herbs, vinegar, oil, and garlic, plus salt and freshly ground black pepper to taste. Grill vegetables on the rack of an uncovered grill directly over medium heat for 8 to 12 minutes or until vegetables are crisp-tender, turning once and brushing occasionally with some of the oil mixture. Transfer vegetables to serving dish; toss with remaining oil mixture.

Nutrition facts per serving: 116 cal., 7 g total fat (1 g sat. fat), 0 mg chol., 39 mg sodium, 13 g carbo., 3 g fiber, 1 g pro. Daily values: 27% vit. A, 112% vit. C, 1% calcium, 6% iron

Note: If desired, substitute 1 small regular eggplant for the Japanese eggplants. Slice the eggplant and grill as above. Before serving, cut the eggplant slices into quarters.

eggplant ideas

One of the best ways to prepare eggplant is to grill it, and there's a multitude of ways to use it once the smoky slices come off the grill. Cut it in small chunks and toss it with warm pasta and feta cheese or with rice, garlic, olive oil, and your favorite herbs to make a chilled salad. Roll strips of it in softened lavosh or pita with goat cheese and grilled red sweet peppers and onions, or simply lay a slice on grilled bread and top it with hummus.

- 3 tablespoons snipped fresh herbs (basil, oregano, and/or parsley)
- 3 tablespoons balsamic vinegar
- 2 tablespoons olive oil
- 2 cloves garlic, minced
- 3 Japanese eggplants, sliced lengthwise ¼ inch thick (about 12 ounces)*
- 2 medium red sweet peppers, seeded and cut into 1-inch-wide strips
- 2 medium sweet onions (such as Vidalia or Walla Walla), sliced ½ inch thick

grilled corn relish

Terrific as a side dish for grilled chicken or pork, this colorful corn relish also makes a light meal stirred with some cooked black beans, rolled up with some shredded Monterey Jack cheese in a flour tortilla, then warmed on the grill.

81

Prep: 15 minutes   Grill: 25 minutes   Makes 4 servings

In medium bowl combine lime juice, oil, and garlic. Brush corn lightly with juice mixture. Sprinkle corn with chili powder. Grill corn on the rack of an uncovered grill directly over medium heat for 25 to 30 minutes or until tender, turning occasionally.

Meanwhile, add avocado, sweet pepper, cilantro, and salt to remaining lime juice mixture; toss well. Cut corn kernels from cob; stir into avocado mixture.

Nutrition facts per serving: 159 cal., 12 g total fat (2 g sat. fat), 0 mg chol., 152 mg sodium, 15 g carbo., 3 g fiber, 3 g pro. Daily values: 15% vit. A, 51% vit. C, 1% calcium, 6% iron

- 3 **tablespoons lime juice**
- 1 **tablespoon cooking oil**
- 2 **cloves garlic, minced**
- 2 **fresh ears of corn, husked and cleaned**
- 1 **teaspoon chili powder**
- 1 **small avocado, seeded, peeled, and cut up**
- ½ **cup chopped red sweet pepper**
- ¼ **cup snipped fresh cilantro**
- ¼ **teaspoon salt**

all about **avocados**

Silky, buttery-tasting avocados are the base of that famous Mexican condiment, guacamole. Before buying avocados, think about how you'll be using them. Firm-ripe avocados are ideal for slicing and chopping; very ripe fruit is perfect for guacamole and mashing in recipes. Buy very firm avocados if you won't be using them for a few days. They'll ripen at room temperature in 3 to 4 days. Avocados peel most easily when they're firm-ripe. Simply cut them in half (moving the knife around the seed), remove the seed, then peel the halves. For a very ripe avocado being used for mashing, just halve the avocado and scoop the pulp away from the skin.

sweets on
the heat

nectarine-raspberry crisp

Chock-full of juicy nectarines and jewel-toned raspberries, this juicy crisp takes full advantage of the best of summer's sweet fruits. If you're pressed for time, assemble it up to 6 hours ahead, then chill until it's time to put it on the grill.

Prep: 15 minutes   Grill: 20 minutes   Makes 6 servings

In a large bowl combine granulated sugar, 2 tablespoons of the flour, the lemon juice, and ¼ teaspoon of the apple pie spice. Gently stir in nectarines and raspberries. Transfer to an 8½×1½-inch round disposable foil baking pan. For the topping, combine the remaining flour, remaining apple pie spice, the brown sugar, and rolled oats. Using a pastry cutter, cut in butter until mixture resembles coarse crumbs. Stir in nuts. Sprinkle topping evenly over fruit mixture.

In a grill with a cover arrange preheated coals in a donut-shape, leaving a 9-inch circle in the center without coals. Test for medium-low heat over the center. Place crisp in pan on center of the grill rack. Cover and grill for 20 to 25 minutes or until fruit mixture is bubbly in center. If desired, serve warm with ice cream.

Nutrition facts per serving: 291 cal., 13 g total fat (5 g sat. fat), 20 mg chol., 80 mg sodium, 45 g carbo., 4 g fiber, 3 g pro. Daily values: 17% vit. A, 23% vit. C, 2% calcium, 8% iron

⅓ cup granulated sugar

5 tablespoons all-purpose flour

1 tablespoon lemon juice

1¼ teaspoons apple pie spice or ground nutmeg

6 medium nectarines (about 2 pounds), pitted and cut into 1-inch chunks

1 cup fresh raspberries

¼ cup packed brown sugar

¼ cup rolled oats

¼ cup cold butter

⅓ cup pecans, coarsely chopped

Vanilla ice cream (optional)

grilled fruit kabobs
with lime-yogurt sauce

When you've got a taste for a little something sweet after a hearty meal, these light and refreshing fruit kabobs are a natural choice. Save the leftovers—if there are any—for a breakfast treat with muffins or cereal the next morning.

6 6- to 8-inch bamboo skewers

1 8-ounce carton vanilla low-fat yogurt

1 teaspoon grated lime peel

1 tablespoon lime juice

¼ teaspoon ground cinnamon

1 small peeled and cored fresh pineapple

2 large ripe, yet firm, nectarines or peeled peaches

2 medium ripe, yet firm, bananas

1 tablespoon melted margarine or butter

2 teaspoons lime juice

Prep: 15 minutes   Grill: 8 minutes   Makes 6 servings

Soak the skewers in warm water for several minutes. Meanwhile, for the sauce, in a small bowl combine the yogurt, lime peel, the 1 tablespoon lime juice, and the cinnamon. Cover and refrigerate until serving time.

For the kabobs, slice pineapple 1 inch thick; quarter slices. Cut nectarines or peeled peaches into wedges. Cut bananas into chunks. Alternately thread pieces of fruit on the skewers. In a small bowl combine melted margarine and the 2 teaspoons lime juice. Brush over kabobs. Grill on the rack of an uncovered grill directly over medium heat for 8 to 10 minutes, turning once or twice. Serve kabobs with the sauce.

Nutrition facts per serving: 161 cal., 3 g total fat (1 g sat. fat), 2 mg chol., 43 mg sodium, 33 g carbo., 2 g fiber, 3 g pro. Daily values: 6% vit. A, 39% vit. C, 5% calcium, 3% iron

desperation **dessert** ideas
If you're short on time, don't desert dessert. Here are some quick ideas:
- Ice cream or sorbet topped with fresh fruit.
- Fresh fruit tossed with honey and sprinkled with toasted nuts (pecans or almonds are good choices).
- Half of a small ripe melon filled with raspberries and topped with vanilla yogurt and toasted almonds.
- A coffee or tea bar that offers a variety of embellishments (for coffee, whipped cream and shaved chocolate; for tea, lemon, sugar, and milk) and purchased biscotti, shortbread, or tea biscuits.

grilled chocolate-raspberry burritos

Chocolate on the grill may sound like a mess, but when it's wrapped up in a tortilla with fresh raspberries, it's anything but. Kids will love this dessert—and can help make it, too. (They'll stay sticky-finger free!) Try it with a scoop of vanilla ice cream.

Prep: 12 minutes   Grill: 8 minutes   Makes 4 servings

Stack the tortillas and wrap in a piece of foil; grill over medium-low heat about 5 minutes or until warm and pliable, turning packet once. [Or, wrap the tortilla stack in microwave-safe paper towels instead of foil; microwave on 100% power (high) for 20 to 40 seconds or until tortillas are warm and pliable.]

Sprinkle ¼ cup each of the chocolate pieces and the raspberries in the center of each tortilla; fold in sides and roll up. Brush burritos with half of the melted butter. Grill burritos on the rack of an uncovered grill directly over medium-low heat about 3 minutes or until the tortillas begin to show grill marks and the chocolate is melted, turning once. Transfer to a serving platter. Brush tortillas with remaining melted butter. In a small bowl combine the sugar and cinnamon; sprinkle over the burritos. Serve immediately.

Nutrition facts per serving: 361 cal., 20 g total fat (4 g sat. fat), 15 mg chol., 179 mg sodium, 49 g carbo., 2 g fiber, 4 g pro. Daily values: 6% vit. A, 12% vit. C, 4% calcium, 15% iron

4 **8- to 9-inch flour tortillas**

1 **cup semisweet chocolate pieces**

1 **cup fresh raspberries**

2 **tablespoons butter, melted**

2 **teaspoons sugar**

½ **teaspoon ground cinnamon**

bananas suzette over grilled pound cake

Here is all the drama of crepes suzette without laboring over the crepes—and no chafing dish required! This elegant dessert is made easily in a skillet right on your grill. For company, garnish each slice with a few delicate strands of orange peel.

Prep: 10 minutes   Grill: 8 minutes   Makes 4 servings

Peel bananas; bias-slice each banana into 8 pieces. Place an 8-inch skillet* on the rack of an uncovered grill directly over medium heat for 2 minutes or until hot. Add the sugar, liqueur, juice, and butter. Heat 1 minute or until butter melts and sugar begins to dissolve. Add the bananas and heat about 4 minutes more or until bananas are just tender, stirring once. Stir in the ⅛ teaspoon nutmeg. Set skillet to the side of the grill rack. Grill pound cake slices on rack of uncovered grill for 1 minute or until golden brown, turning once.

To serve, spoon bananas and sauce over pound cake slices. If desired, garnish with shredded orange peel and additional nutmeg.

Nutrition facts per serving: 292 cal., 12 g total fat (7 g sat. fat), 67 mg chol., 139 mg sodium, 42 g carbo., 1 g fiber, 3 g pro. Daily values: 12% vit. A, 15% vit. C, 2% calcium, 5% iron

*Note: The heat from the grill will blacken the outside of the skillet, so use a cast-iron or old skillet.

- 2 **medium ripe, yet firm, bananas**
- 3 **tablespoons sugar**
- 2 **tablespoons orange-flavored liqueur**
- 2 **tablespoons orange juice**
- 1 **tablespoon butter**
- ⅛ **teaspoon ground nutmeg**
- ½ **of a 10¾-ounce package frozen pound cake, thawed and cut into 4 slices**
- **Shredded orange peel (optional)**
- **Ground nutmeg (optional)**

hazelnut pears

Sweet, ripe pears are cooked in a cardamom-spiced caramel sauce studded with toasted hazelnuts that's perfect with ice cream or shortcake. Prepare the foil-pack along with dinner, then toss it on the grill while you eat for a sweet and easy finish.

⅓ cup packed brown sugar

2 tablespoons butter, softened

2 tablespoons light corn syrup

¼ teaspoon ground nutmeg

¼ teaspoon ground cardamom

3 cups cored sliced pears (3 medium)

⅓ cup chopped toasted hazelnuts

   Vanilla ice cream (optional)

Prep: 30 minutes   Grill: 15 minutes   Makes 4 to 6 servings

In a small bowl combine brown sugar, softened butter, corn syrup, nutmeg, and cardamom. Set aside. Tear off a 36x18-inch piece of heavy foil. Fold in half to make a double thickness of foil that measures 18x18 inches. Place pear slices in the center of the foil. Spoon brown sugar mixture atop pears. Sprinkle with nuts. Bring up two opposite edges of foil and seal with a double fold. Fold ends to completely enclose the pears, leaving space for steam to build. Place foil packet on grill rack of an uncovered grill directly over medium coals for 12 to 15 minutes or until pears are tender. Serve warm pear mixture with ice cream, if desired. Makes 4 to 6 servings.

Nutrition facts per serving: 289 cal., 14 g total fat (4 g sat. fat), 15 mg chol., 163 mg sodium, 43 g carbo., 5 g fiber, 2 g pro. Daily values: 5% vit. A, 8% vit. C, 4% calcium, 9% iron

grilled pineapple with sugared wontons

Get under blue skies and into a slower pace with each bite of this tropical dessert. Juicy, rum-glazed, grilled pineapple is sprinkled with a touch of coconut and a whimsical embellishment: wonton skins crisped on the grill and sprinkled with sugar.

Prep: 10 minutes   Grill: 10 minutes   Makes 4 servings

Place pineapple in a single layer in a shallow dish. In a small bowl stir together the brown sugar, vinegar, rum, and lime juice until sugar dissolves. Pour brown sugar mixture over the pineapple; set aside. Place a sheet of waxed paper on a cookie sheet. Lay wonton wrappers on waxed paper. Brush both sides with melted butter. Put coconut in a disposable foil pie pan or on a double thickness of heavy foil.

Drain pineapple, reserving brown sugar mixture. Grill pineapple on the rack of an uncovered grill directly over medium heat for 6 to 8 minutes, turning once and brushing occasionally with some of the reserved brown sugar mixture. Transfer pineapple to serving bowls. Place the wonton wrappers directly on the grill rack; grill for 2 to 4 minutes or until browned, using tongs to turn once. Return the grilled wontons to the cookie sheet; immediately sprinkle with the granulated sugar. Transfer the pie pan or foil with the coconut to the grill. Using a pair of tongs, shake pan or foil back and forth about 2 minutes or until coconut is lightly toasted. Drizzle the remaining brown sugar mixture over pineapple; sprinkle with coconut and serve with sugared wontons.

Nutrition facts per serving: 204 cal., 5 g total fat (3 g sat. fat), 9 mg chol., 103 mg sodium, 38 g carbo., 2 g fiber, 2 g pro. Daily values: 2% vit. A, 32% vit. C, 2% calcium, 8% iron

6 ¾-inch-thick slices peeled and cored fresh pineapple, quartered

¼ cup packed brown sugar

2 tablespoons rice vinegar or seasoned rice vinegar

2 tablespoons rum

4 teaspoons lime juice

6 wonton wrappers, halved diagonally

1 tablespoon butter, melted

3 tablespoons shredded coconut

1 tablespoon granulated sugar

poultry

If desired, remove the skin from the poultry. Rinse poultry and pat dry with paper towels. Test for desired coal temperature (see tip, page 36). Place poultry on the grill rack, bone side up, directly over the preheated coals (for direct grilling) or directly over drip pan (for indirect grilling). Grill (uncovered for direct grilling or covered for indirect grilling) for the time given below or until tender and no longer pink. (Note: White meat will cook slightly faster.) Turn poultry over halfway through the grilling time.

Type of Bird	Weight	Temperature	Doneness	Direct Grilling* Time	Indirect Grilling* Time
Chicken, broiler-fryer, half	1¼ to 1½ pounds	Medium	Tender; no longer pink	40 to 50 minutes	1 to 1¼ hours
Chicken breast half, skinned and boned	4 to 5 ounces each	Medium	Tender; no longer pink	12 to 15 minute	15 to 18 minutes
Chicken quarters	2½ to 3 pounds total	Medium	Tender; no longer pink	40 to 50 minutes	50 to 60 minutes
Meaty chicken pieces	2 to 2½ pounds total	Medium	Tender; no longer pink	35 to 45 minutes	50 to 60 minutes
Turkey breast tenderloin steak	4 to 6 ounces each	Medium	Tender; no longer pink	12 to 15 minutes	15 to 18 minutes

*Note: Most of the recipes in this book are grilled by direct heat, unless otherwise noted. For differences in methods, see tip on page 54.

beef, pork, or lamb

Test for the desired temperature (see tip, page 36). Place the meat on the rack of a grill directly over the preheated coals (for direct grilling) or directly over a drip pan (for indirect grilling). Grill meat (uncovered for direct grilling or covered for indirect grilling) for the time given below or until done, turning the meat over halfway through the grilling time.

Cut	Thickness	Temperature	Doneness	Direct Grilling* Time	Indirect Grilling* Time
Beef					
Boneless sirloin steak	1 inch	Medium	Medium rare	14 to 18 minutes	22 to 26 minutes
			Medium	18 to 22 minutes	26 to 30 minutes
	1½ inches	Medium	Medium rare	32 to 36 minutes	32 to 36 minutes
			Medium	36 to 40 minutes	36 to 40 minutes
Flank steak	¾ to 1 inch	Medium	Medium	12 to 14 minutes	18 to 22 minutes
Ground meat patties	¾ inch (4 per pound)	Medium	No pink remains	14 to 18 minutes	20 to 24 minutes
Steak (blade, chuck, top round)	1 inch	Medium	Medium rare	14 to 16 minutes	45 to 55 minutes
			Medium	18 to 20 minutes	60 to 70 minutes
	1½ inches	Medium	Medium rare	19 to 26 minutes	50 to 60 minutes
			Medium	27 to 32 minutes	1 to 1¼ hours
Steak (porterhouse, rib, rib eye, sirloin, T-bone, tenderloin, top loin)	1 inch	Medium	Medium rare	8 to 12 minutes	16 to 20 minutes
			Medium	12 to 15 minutes	20 to 24 minutes
	1¼ to 1½ inches	Medium	Medium rare	14 to 18 minutes	20 to 22 minutes
			Medium	18 to 22 minutes	22 to 26 minutes
Pork**					
Chop	¾ inch	Medium	Medium	8 to 11 minutes	20 to 24 minutes
	1¼ to 1½ inches	Medium	Medium	25 to 30 minutes	35 to 40 minutes
Lamb					
Chop	1 inch	Medium	Medium rare	10 to 14 minutes	16 to 18 minutes
		Medium	Medium	14 to 16 minutes	18 to 20 minutes
Kabobs	1-inch cubes	Medium	Medium	12 to 14 minutes	

*Note: Most of the recipes in this book are grilled by direct heat unless otherwise noted. For differences in methods, see tip on page 54.
**Note: Pork should be cooked until juices run clear.

fish & seafood

Thaw fish or shellfish, if frozen. Test for desired temperature (see tip, page 36). For fish fillets, place in a well-greased grill basket. For fish steaks and whole fish, grease the grill rack. Place the fish on the rack directly over the preheated coals (for direct grilling) or over a drip pan (for indirect grilling). Grill (uncovered for direct grilling or covered for indirect grilling), for the time given below or until the fish just begins to flake easily when tested with a fork; scallops and shrimp should look opaque. Turn the fish over halfway through the grilling time. If desired, brush fish with melted margarine or butter.

Form of Fish	Weight, Size, or Thickness	Temperature	Doneness	Direct Grilling* Time	Indirect Grilling* Time
Dressed fish	½ to 1½ pounds	Medium	Flakes	7 to 9 minutes per ½ pound	20 to 25 minutes per ½ pound
Fillets, steaks, cubes (for kabobs)	½ to 1 inch thick	Medium	Flakes	4 to 6 minutes per ½-inch thickness	4 to 6 minutes per ½-inch thickness
Sea scallops (for kabobs)	(12 to 15 per pound)	Medium	Opaque	5 to 8 minutes	5 to 7 minutes
Shrimp (for kabobs)	Medium (20 per pound)	Medium	Opaque	6 to 8 minutes	6 to 8 minutes
	Jumbo (12 to 15 per pound)	Medium	Opaque	10 to 12 minutes	8 to 10 minutes

*Note: Most of the of the recipes in this book are grilled by direct heat unless otherwise noted. For differences in methods, see tip on page 54.

vegetables

Before grilling, rinse, trim, cut up, and precook vegetables as directed below. To precook vegetables, in a saucepan bring a small amount of water to boiling; add desired vegetable and simmer, covered, for the time specified in the chart. Drain well. Generously brush vegetables with olive oil, margarine, or butter before grilling to prevent vegetables from sticking to the grill rack. Test for desired temperature (see tip, page 36).

To grill, place vegetables on a piece of heavy foil or on the grill rack directly over the preheated coals. If putting vegetables directly on grill rack, lay them perpendicular to wires of the rack so they won't fall into the coals. Grill, uncovered, for the time given below or until tender, turning occasionally. Monitor the grilling closely so vegetables don't char.

93

Vegetable	Preparation	Precooking Time	Direct-Grilling* Time
Asparagus	Snap off and discard tough bases of stems. Precook, then tie asparagus in bundles with strips of cooked green onion tops.	3 to 4 minutes	3 to 5 minutes
Corn on the cob	Remove husks from corn. Scrub ears with a stiff brush to remove silks. Rinse corn; pat dry.	Do not precook	20 to 30 minutes
Eggplant	Cut off top and blossom ends. Cut eggplant crosswise into 1-inch-thick slices.	Do not precook	8 minutes
Fennel	Snip off feathery leaves. Cut off stems.	10 minutes, then cut into 6 to 8 wedges	8 minutes
Fresh baby carrots	Cut off carrot tops. Wash and peel carrots.	3 to 5 minutes	3 to 5 minutes
Leeks	Cut off green tops. Rinse well; trim bulb roots and remove 1 or 2 layers of white skin.	10 minutes or until tender; then halve lengthwise	5 minutes
New potatoes	Halve potatoes.	10 minutes or until almost tender	10 to 12 minutes
Pattypan squash	Rinse; trim ends.	3 minutes	20 minutes
Sweet peppers	Remove stems. Quarter peppers. Remove seeds and membranes. Cut into 1-inch-wide strips.	Do not precook	8 to 10 minutes
Zucchini or yellow summer squash	Wash; cut off ends. Quarter lengthwise.	Do not precook	5 to 6 minutes

*Note: Because vegetables contain little fat to drip off, they don't require a drip pan. Therefore, timings are given for direct grilling only.

METRIC COOKING HINTS

By making a few conversions, cooks in Australia, Canada, and the United Kingdom can use the recipes in *Better Homes and Gardens* ® *Fresh and Simple*™ *Casual Cookouts* with confidence. The charts on this page provide a guide for converting measurements from the U.S. customary system, which is used throughout this book, to the imperial and metric systems. There also is a conversion table for oven temperatures to accommodate the differences in oven calibrations.

Product Differences: Most of the ingredients called for in the recipes in this book are available in English-speaking countries. However, some are known by different names. Here are some common American ingredients and their possible counterparts:

- Sugar is granulated or castor sugar.
- Powdered sugar is icing sugar.
- All-purpose flour is plain household flour or white flour. When self-rising flour is used in place of all-purpose flour in a recipe that calls for leavening, omit the leavening agent (baking soda or baking powder) and salt.
- Light-colored corn syrup is golden syrup.
- Cornstarch is cornflour.
- Baking soda is bicarbonate of soda.
- Vanilla is vanilla essence.
- Green, red, or yellow sweet peppers are capsicums.
- Golden raisins are sultanas.

Volume and Weight: Americans traditionally use cup measures for liquid and solid ingredients. The chart, above right, shows the approximate imperial and metric equivalents. If you are accustomed to weighing solid ingredients, the following approximate equivalents will be helpful.

- 1 cup butter, castor sugar, or rice = 8 ounces = about 250 grams
- 1 cup flour = 4 ounces = about 125 grams
- 1 cup icing sugar = 5 ounces = about 150 grams

Spoon measures are used for smaller amounts of ingredients. Although the size of the tablespoon varies slightly in different countries, for practical purposes and for recipes in this book, a straight substitution is all that's necessary.

Measurements made using cups or spoons always should be level unless stated otherwise.

Equivalents: U.S. = Australia/U.K./Canada

⅛ teaspoon = 0.5 ml
¼ teaspoon = 1 ml
½ teaspoon = 2 ml
1 teaspoon = 5 ml
1 tablespoon = 1 tablespoon
¼ cup = 2 tablespoons = 2 fluid ounces = 60 ml
⅓ cup = ¼ cup = 3 fluid ounces = 90 ml
½ cup = ⅓ cup = 4 fluid ounces = 120 ml
⅔ cup = ½ cup = 5 fluid ounces = 150 ml
¾ cup = ⅔ cup = 6 fluid ounces = 180 ml
1 cup = ¾ cup = 8 fluid ounces = 240 ml
1¼ cups = 1 cup
2 cups = 1 pint
1 quart = 1 liter
½ inch = 1.27 cm
1 inch = 2.54 cm

Baking Pan Sizes

American	Metric
8×1½-inch round baking pan	20×4-cm cake tin
9×1½-inch round baking pan	23×3.5-cm cake tin
11×7×1½-inch baking pan	28×18×4-cm baking tin
13×9×2-inch baking pan	30×20×3-cm baking tin
2-quart rectangular baking dish	30×20×3-cm baking tin
15×10×1-inch baking pan	30×25×2-cm baking tin (Swiss roll tin)
9-inch pie plate	22×4- or 23×4-cm pie plate
7- or 8-inch springform pan	18- or 20-cm springform or loose-bottom cake tin
9×5×3-inch loaf pan	23×13×7-cm or 2-pound narrow loaf tin or pâté tin
1½-quart casserole	1.5-liter casserole
2-quart casserole	2-liter casserole

Oven Temperature Equivalents

Fahrenheit Setting	Celsius Setting*	Gas Setting
300°F	150°C	Gas Mark 2 (slow)
325°F	160°C	Gas Mark 3 (moderately slow)
350°F	180°C	Gas Mark 4 (moderate)
375°F	190°C	Gas Mark 5 (moderately hot)
400°F	200°C	Gas Mark 6 (hot)
425°F	220°C	Gas Mark 7
450°F	230°C	Gas Mark 8 (very hot)
Broil		Grill

*Electric and gas ovens may be calibrated using Celsius. However, for an electric oven, increase the Celsius setting 10 to 20 degrees when cooking above 160°C. For convection or forced-air ovens (gas or electric), lower the temperature setting 10°C when cooking at all heat levels.

Better Homes and Gardens®
fresh and **simple**™

casual cookouts

Cook your whole meal on the grill using *Casual Cookouts* as your guide. With every recipe ready in about 30 minutes, even grillers on the go can enjoy these open-air menus any night of the week.

Creativity: The big promise behind *Casual Cookouts* is flavor. You won't find the usual grilled goods or gourmet-takes-days-to-make dishes. Every recipe pairs the freshest ingredients with innovative seasonings and the promise of ease, offering results that make firing up the grill worth it—night after night.

Convenience: Once the coals are hot, grab a chair and relax. Every recipe, from entrées to sides and desserts, is grilled so you won't need to keep running indoors and out.

Ease: Proof is on the grill that dinners such as Jerk London Broil, Grilled Vietnamese Chicken Breasts, and Turkey Burgers with Fresh Curry Catsup are a real breeze. Menu suggestions that appear with every entrée keep the planning simple, too.